BELONGING TO 2 TROOP

Robbie Burns

What makes the best units fight? This intimate account makes it clear that it is not, king, country, or cause, but the bonds built with those to the left and right of you, the sense of 'belonging'. As GOC 3 (UK) Division I had 9 Parachute Squadron Royal Engineers under command. Frankly, they were a bit of a nightmare in peace. As this memoir shows they were also extraordinary soldiers in war. They were some of the very best troops in the British Army, which means any army, and this moving story of 2 Troop explains why.

General Sir John McColl KCB CBE DSO
Deputy Supreme Allied Commander, Europe. 2007–2011

An evocative, uplifting and very personal account of a Royal Engineer Parachute Troop who helped recapture the Falkland Islands in 1982 after the Argentine invasion, superbly told by Robbie Burns, their Troop Commander. His descriptions of the fighting and the challenging conditions that he and his men faced are very sobering, but what shines through the book is their exceptional quality, both as soldiers and human beings. Their strong bonds of brotherhood are inspiring. This is an enthralling story.

Brigadier (Retired) Ian McGill CBE
Engineer-in-Chief, (Army). 1995–1998

This is an exceptional piece of writing about a special parachute engineer troop in a unique time in our shared history. 40 years on, Robbie Burns has written a personal and touching account in "Belonging to 2 Troop" that brings out the courage, toughness, professionalism and compassion of this galant band of parachute engineers. They were plucked from their home squadron and cast into the cauldron of the Falklands campaign from the very start, fighting as combat engineers, right through to the end.

Robbie writes with clarity of the bond felt between the troop members as well as the need they all felt to be a recognized and appreciated as part of a larger team. His description, after the losses of Mount Longdon, of the humanity afforded to Argentine prisoners there, and during their transit by ship back to Argentina, is important and something for which we should all be rightly proud. This is remembered, with gratitude, by Argentine veterans to this day.

This is a wonderful, well written story. Robbie and 2 Troop brought honour to themselves and 9 Parachute Squadron. I could not have been prouder to serve with them. I treasure the friendship we share to this day.

Brigadier (Retd) Roderick Macdonald MBE
Officer Commanding 59 Independent Commando
Squadron Royal Engineers
3 Commando Brigade Royal Marines 1982

BELONGING TO 2 TROOP

A MEMOIR OF THE FALKLANDS WAR 1982

Brigadier (Retired) Robbie Burns OBE

Riverside Publishing Solutions

Copyright © 2022 Robbie Burns

All rights reserved. No part of this publication may be reproduced, stored in a database or retrieval system, or transmitted, in any form or by any means, without the prior permission in writing of the author, nor be otherwise circulated in any form or binding or cover other than that in which it is published and without a similar condition including this condition being imposed on the subsquent purchaser.

The majority of the images in this book
are from the author's collection.

Every attempt has been made to gain permission for the use of images not from the author's collection in this book. Any omissions will be rectified in future editions.

ISBN (Hardback): 978-1-913012-68-7
ISBN (Paperback): 978-1-913012-69-4
ISBN (ePub): 978-1-913012-70-0

The moral right of the author has been asserted.

A full CIP record for this book is available from the British Library.

First published in 2022 in association with
Riverside Publishing Solutions, Salisbury, UK

www.riversidepublishingsolutions.com

Printed and bound in the UK.

CONTENTS

List of Photographs and Illustrations		vii
Acknowledgements		xiii
Foreword		xvii
Chapter 1	Prologue	1
Chapter 2	2 Troop's preparations	3
Chapter 3	Embarkation	17
Chapter 4	Sailing South	21
Chapter 5	Ascension Island	31
Chapter 6	Into the South Atlantic	35
Chapter 7	A Change of Plan	41
Chapter 8	The Landings at Port San Carlos	45
Chapter 9	The First Week Ashore	57
Chapter 10	Blue on Blue	63
Chapter 11	The March East	73
Chapter 12	Estancia	81
Chapter 13	Mount Longdon	91
Chapter 14	Port Stanley	111
Chapter 15	Billy's Story	117
Chapter 16	The Home Front	123
Chapter 17	The Return Home	135
Chapter 18	Reflections	141
References		*143*
2 Troop, 9 Parachute Squadron Royal Engineers Orbat		*145*

LIST OF PHOTOGRAPHS, MAPS AND ILLUSTRATIONS

1. 2 Troop, 9 Parachute Squadron, Royal Engineers, February 1982.   11

2. A letter from Lieutenant Colonel 'H' Jones, CO 2 Para to Lieutenant Colonel Geoff Field, CO 36 Engineer Regiment, thanking 2 Troop for their efforts in Kenya in November and December 1981.   12

3. The Band of the Parachute Regiment play at the quayside in Portsmouth as MV Norland casts off with 2 Para Group embarked.   13

4. Wives and girlfriends on the quayside to say farewell, Portsmouth.   13

5. MV Norland heading South, April 1982.   14

6. SS Canberra. 2 Troop was airlifted onto Canberra 3 days before the landings at San Carlos.   14

7. Lieutenant Colonels Hew Pike (3 Para) and 'H' Jones (2 Para) standing on the flight deck of the SS Canberra at Ascension Island. 2 Troop sailed with 2 Para but cross decked to support 3 Para for the invasion.   15

8.	Members of 2 Troop prepare to be cross decked from the MV Norland onto SS Canberra. Pictured (Left to Right) are Derek Broadbent, Kev Lillicrap, Taff Sweeney, Pete Guerin, John Hare and Scott Wilson.	47
9.	HMS Intrepid. 2 Troop went ashore from Intrepid via LCVP.	48
10.	2 Troop about to go ashore at Port San Carlos on D-Day.	48
11.	Soup being served to members of 3 Para on the 21st of May. A whale jaw stands behind the group at Port San Carlos settlement.	49
12.	Troop headquarters trench at Port San Carlos.	49
13.	Tea being offered to Willy Macdonald.	50
14.	Staff Sergeant Pete Guerin digging in.	50
15.	Jock Ferry in pensive mood.	51
16.	On guard duty during one of the many air attacks.	51
17.	Map showing the landings on the 21st of May and the enemy positions on Fanning Head.	70
18.	A 105mm Light Gun from 7 (Sphinx) Battery. Around 82 rounds were fired at the A Company patrol in the 23rd of May blue-on-blue incident.	71

LIST OF PHOTOGRAPHS, MAPS AND ILLUSTRATIONS

19. Casualties from the blue-on-blue incident were initially flown onto HMS Intrepid, before being transferred to the field surgical facility at Ajax Bay. 71

20. Surgeon Commander Rick Jolly outside the surgical facility at Ajax Bay. Every casualty who made it to his surgery survived. 72

21. The author – 'Troopie', during the march to Estancia. 85

22. Steve Wildman, Scott Wilson and the author check out their feet. 86

23. A break from the march to Estancia. 86

24. Corporal Scott Wilson. 87

25. 11th June. Final preparations for the Battle for Mount Longdon. 88

26. 11th June. Final Preparations for the Battle for Mount Longdon. 88

27. RFA Sir Galahad, following the air attack. 8th June 1982 89

28. Map of 3 Para's route from Port San Carlos to Port Stanley. 103

29. Map of Mount Longdon, 11th–12th June 1982. 103

30. First aid being administered to Argentine casualties. 104

31.	Argentine prisoners of war under guard.	104
32.	Prisoners of war being searched for weapons.	105
33.	12th June. Mick Humphries manages a grim smile.	105
34.	Casualties being assembled at the Regimental Aid Post for helicopter evacuation.	106
35.	Mick Leather with the Troop's 30mm machine gun. (This could be an Argentinian 50mm Browning captured on Mount Longdon)	106
36.	Five members of the Troop shortly before the Argentine surrender. Pictured are Sapper Smith, Lance Corporal Moore and Sappers Rodgers, Preston, and Robson.	107
37.	2 Troop hear the news of the Argentine surrender. 14th June 1982.	107
38.	The Troop's first glimpse of Port Stanley from the summit of Mount Longdon.	108
39.	The memorial plaque to Corporal Scott Wilson, on Mount Longdon.	108
40.	Past and present members of 9 Parachute Squadron pay their respects to Scott Wilson on Mount Longdon. Present in the photograph are Freddie Kemp, (Squadron 2ic in 1982), John Hare and Derek Broadbent from 2 Troop (1982).	109

LIST OF PHOTOGRAPHS, MAPS AND ILLUSTRATIONS

41. Billy Morris on board the MV Norland was witness to HMS Antelope sinking in San Carlos water. Norland took on board the Antelope's surviving crew. 122

42. Armed only with a sub machine gun, Billy Morris was tasked with guard duties on MV Norland as the vessel was attacked by Argentine aircraft in San Carlos water. 122

43. Captain Dick Barton, Admin Officer and Families Officer, 9 Parachute Squadron, and his dog, Louey. 131

44. 9 Parachute Squadron wives prepare for their charity parachute jump with the Red Devils, May 1982. 132

45. Jock, Sandra and Gavin Ferry on the bus home to Aldershot from RAF Brize Norton. 133

46. Robbie and Mandy Burns' wedding finally took place on the 7th of August 1982. The guard of honour included Captain Freddie Kemp, 2ic 9 Parachute Squadron, Captain Dick Barton, the Squadron's Families Officer and Captain Richard Willett, 1 Troop Commander. 137

47. Letter written by Major Roddy Macdonald to Lieutenant Colonel Geoff Field, CO 36 Engineer Regiment at the end of hostilities, in June 1982. Although in 1982 this copy was intended

	for the author's personal information only. Roddy Macdonald has agreed that it can be included in this account of 2 Troop's story.	138
48.	Majors Roddy Macdonald, OC 59 Independent Commando Squadron and Chris Davies, OC 9 Parachute Squadron, Royal Engineers. Photo taken on Stanley airfield after the surrender.	139
49.	Taff Sweeny.	147
50.	Jock Ferry.	148
51.	Mick Humphries.	148
52.	Steve (Billy) Morris and Mick Leather.	149
53.	Sandra Ferry and Chris Humphries.	149
54.	Derek Broadbent.	150
55.	Ginge Moore.	150

ACKNOWLEDGEMENTS

In 1980, I was lucky enough to find myself in command of 2 Troop, 9 Parachute Squadron, Royal Engineers. I returned to the Squadron in 1987 as Officer Commanding, and subsequently had the Squadron under command in 1993 when I was appointed Commanding Officer, 36 Engineer Regiment. Although I have done some exciting things both inside and outside the British Army since, my two-year spell commanding 2 Troop were, in many ways, the best years of my life. The 1982 Falklands War saw the Troop deploy to the South Atlantic independently from its parent Squadron. Its story is unique, but undocumented.

I have struggled for 40 years to write an account of 2 Troop's story. Then, in 2019, I was on business in California and was offered a bed for the night at Roddy Macdonald's home in Napa Valley. Roddy was my boss in the Falklands and has remained a close friend ever since. That evening, he finally pinned me down to write something on 2 Troop's experience. Unable to wriggle out of it, I agreed to put pen to paper. So, my thanks go to Roddy for his support and encouragement. Two former Officers Commanding 9 Parachute Squadron, Chris Davies and Ian McGill also read through the account with enthusiasm and a critical eye, which was appreciated.

My thanks also to Taff Sweeney, Jock Ferry and Mick Humphries for giving up their time and helping me recall the events of that summer. They have been unstinting in their support.

Others who have given up their time to help with this account have included Derek Broadbent, Paul Moore, Mick Leather, Billy Morris and Sam Robson, all key members of 2 Troop back in 1982. I have also included sections from Dr AD Chissel's article, 'Friendly Fire in the Falklands', and extracts from James O'Connell's account of the Battle for Mount Longdon, titled 'Three Days in June'. Both these authors have given their blessing to me using their brilliantly researched material.

A special mention goes to Jean Wilson, whose personal sacrifice cannot be measured. I am so grateful to her for agreeing to be interviewed for this memoir. Thanks also to Sandra Ferry and Chris Humphries, who were kind enough to help me provide an insight into what life was like for the wives and the bereaved back home in Aldershot during the summer of 1982. I should also thank Dick Barton, who looked after the wives as Squadron Rear Party and Families Officer that summer, and who proof read that section for me.

I have tried to relate what the Troop was doing with the sequence of events at the broader political and strategic levels. 'The bigger picture' is dealt with in short paragraphs of fact in bold indented text. These paragraphs appear in chronological order as events unfolded in 1982.

I fully recognise that this account is but one version of the truth. Others will have very different recollections.

ACKNOWLEDGEMENTS

I kick myself that I did not keep a diary worthy of the name during the conflict. As a consequence, there are parts of the story that have had to be reconstructed from a distillation of others' memories. For that I can only apologise. I hope this account goes someway to telling our story.

I have another reason for writing this account. At the time, my reputation as the Troop Commander was one of being rather intense, and of dealing out rather more criticism than praise. 'Too much stick and not enough carrot boss' was one comment I received at the time. Indeed, when I think back, I cannot recall properly thanking everyone for their unbelievable efforts as we finally returned home. But now, my recollections are ones of immense pride in what we collectively achieved. It was a great honour to be part of this Band of Brothers. I hope this account goes at least part of the way to redressing that situation.

My heartfelt thanks go to all members of that special group of soldiers, 2 Troop, 9 Parachute Squadron.

Robbie Burns
April 2022

Dedicated to the Memory of Corporal Scott Wilson

FOREWORD

As the Commander of 3 Commando Brigade in the Falklands War, I counted myself very fortunate to have the support of 59 Independent Commando Squadron, Royal Engineers, commanded by Roddy Macdonald. The Squadron was re-enforced by a large and capable troop from 9 Parachute Squadron. This was good news for three reasons. Firstly, they were tough and uncompromising soldiers who fitted in with the ethos of my brigade. Secondly, they were also well respected by the officers and men of the two Parachute battalions re-enforcing the brigade. And thirdly, they were, of course, highly capable field engineers.

This account follows the story of their preparations and their journey South, first on the MV Norland, and subsequently in SS Canberra and HMS Intrepid. It follows them as they landed at Port San Carlos on D-Day, and traces their steps as they yomped (or rather tabbed) across East Falklands, supported 3 Para on Mount Longdon, and finally helped return Port Stanley to normality after the war. Their Troop Commander, Robbie Burns, also picks up the story of the wives back in Aldershot and how they coped in the summer of 1982.

Robbie Burns writes perceptively enabling the reader to get a real feel for the personalities of the soldiers and what they endured. What comes across very clearly is not only their professionalism, their resolve and their determination, but also the importance of small unit morale when presented with extreme challenges. Belonging to 2 Troop mattered to this small band of sappers in 1982. I suspect it still matters to them today.

I was delighted when I heard that a troop from 9 Parachute Squadron was to join my Brigade. I had soldiers from this squadron under command in Northern Ireland some years before and knew that they would perform splendidly in the Falklands. They more than fulfilled my expectations.

Red and Green berets have been comrades in arms in many a strife, and despite the keen rivalry that exists between them, I know that I speak for all wearers of the green beret when I say that there is no one I would rather fight alongside than soldiers wearing a red beret.

Major General Julian Thompson

'In war, which is an intense form of life, Chance casts aside all veils and disguises and presents herself nakedly from moment to moment as the direct arbiter over all persons and events.'

Winston Churchill, Thoughts and Adventures

Chapter 1

PROLOGUE

This is a story about belonging. It traces the events of a small group of soldiers over a four-month period in the summer of 1982. We were engineers as well as parachute trained soldiers; some married, most single, all committed to the cause. The war we fought in was a just war in our eyes, and so we needed no convincing about the rights and wrongs of it. However, when we were sent 8,000 miles from home, into the South Atlantic, we were not only separated from family and friends, but also from our parent organisation which would, under normal circumstances, have provided leadership, guidance, information and sustenance. Things were compounded as we prepared to fight the land battle. Late re-organisations amongst the amphibious landing force left us friendless as we went ashore. How we coped in such circumstances is at the heart of our story.

Chapter 2

2 TROOP'S PREPARATIONS

On Thursday 1st April 1982, 2 Troop, 9 Parachute Squadron was 35 strong. It was April Fool's Day! We were to be found training at Longmoor Ranges in Hampshire. It was a typical Spring day with the weather finally improving and a bit of heat in the sun lifting spirits. In many ways it was also a typical day's training: a march to the range, a rifle practice shoot using our 7.62mm Self Loading Rifles, and a truck journey back to barracks. Life was good for 2 Troop. We were looking forward to a summer of parachuting, combat engineering, fitness training and sport. The next day, Friday the 2nd of April involved only a morning's parachuting from the balloon on Queens Avenue, Aldershot before we departed for Easter leave. News on the radio the following day was to change all this.

One of four troops which comprised the fiercely proud airborne engineer sub-unit, 2 Troop had recently seen service in Kenya with 2nd Battalion, the Parachute Regiment, and prior to that, in Denmark on NATO exercises and in Northern Ireland, on a five-month operational tour. The Squadron had earned and sustained a reputation for robustness, resilience and tenacity, even amongst the tough airborne community in Aldershot. But it was equally capable of indiscipline if not being fully entertained by demanding training exercises or operations.

Commanding 2 Troop was a unique experience. The sappers were generally a couple of years older than their infantry counterparts. They were highly intelligent and trained as both soldiers and engineers. Their parachute training placed them as a breed apart. In the early 1980s, only about 1 in 4 of those who volunteered for Parachute training passed P Company, the physical selection course. Non parachute trained soldiers were known as 'craphats' and were either ignored or derided by Squadron members. The NCOs were mature: more mature than me, and they were thinkers and fixers. They knew what could realistically be achieved and they knew the strengths and weaknesses of each member of the Troop. I would have been an idiot not to consult widely before agreeing a course of action.

In recent years, I have had civilian friends suggest that commanding soldiers must have been easy …'all you had to do is order them to do something, and they went away and did it'. I don't remember being a young officer commanding 2 Troop as anything like that. Firstly, without the credentials of earning my parachute wings, I would have found my position untenable. No-one would have listened to me. Secondly, for the most part, my role was to facilitate success by making sure that the guys had the right equipment, stores, transport or weapons. Once provided with the tools for the job, they needed

CHAPTER 2

very little encouragement. Commanding 2 Troop often felt like riding a thoroughbred horse. The challenge was rarely about getting them to do something, but more about keeping them pointing in the right direction and putting the brakes on at the right time.

In the months prior to our Falklands deployment, we had been heavily involved in supporting our new formation, 5 Infantry Brigade, which had just been formed. Commanded by Brigadier Tony Wilson, the Brigade had a Priority 1 Home Defence role, with a more exciting and glamorous Priority 2 role of being capable and ready to deploy anywhere outside the NATO area. In early 1982, the Brigade comprised three infantry battalions including 2 and 3 Para, as well as 36 Engineer Regiment providing engineer support. But it had no artillery, armour or intrinsic logistic support so was poorly placed to conduct effective 'Out of Area' operations.

February had been spent at Stamford Training Area in East Anglia with our new Brigade on Exercise 'Green Lanyard'. 9 Squadron also had a new boss. Major Ian McGill had departed on 11th February, and the new Officer Commanding, Chris Davies had taken the helm as we set off for the Brigade exercise. The exercise was preceded by a series of capability demonstrations and for 2 Troop, this involved a booby trap demonstration followed by improvised rafting on Buckingham Tofts lake. We performed well on the final exercise and our new boss liked what he saw. This was important for me because I knew that I had an extraordinary team and didn't want anyone to think less highly of them than I did.

BELONGING TO 2 TROOP

March saw the Troop in Aldershot, training and parachuting, and providing support to the Army Staff College demonstration. We also fielded a significant number of the Squadron rugby team that won the South-East District Minor Units Cup, setting us up nicely for the Army Minor Units Final, a match we never played.

The Falkland Islands lie 400 miles due East of Southern Argentina and 350 miles North-East of Cape Horn. The land mass is 4,700 square miles, just over half the size of Wales. The first known landing on the Falklands Islands was by Captain Strong in 1690, who named Falkland Sound after the then Commissioner of the Admiralty, Lord Falkland. There has been a continuous British presence on the Islands since 1833.

On the 31st of March 1982, UK intelligence sources confirmed that the Falkland Islands would be invaded on the 2nd of April. The intelligence sources were correct. Argentinian Forces occupied the capital, Port Stanley, on the 2nd of April and invaded South Georgia the following day.

On Friday the 2nd of April, back in Plymouth, Brigadier Julian Thompson was woken up to be given the order to prepare 3 Commando Brigade to move South and recapture the Falkland Islands. Two aircraft carriers, HMS Hermes and HMS Invincible were put on 48 hours' notice

CHAPTER 2

to sail South. The next day, the 3rd of April, SS Canberra was requisitioned by the Royal Navy to carry troops South.

On Saturday the 3rd of April 1982, 9 Parachute Squadron was called into barracks in Aldershot. Rhine Barracks was but one element of a hideous concrete barrack complex known as Montgomery Lines, home for 5 Infantry Brigade. The 2nd Battalion, the Parachute Regiment and 216 Parachute Signals Squadron were also based there. That Saturday morning was remembered for a buzz of excitement balanced with an equal measure of disbelief. The four Troops gathered and paraded next to our engineer storerooms which encircled the parade square, with lots of questions being asked. Where was the Falklands? Were they in Scotland? Who lived there? Were they British citizens? What was the Argentinian Army like? Would the British Army be sent to recapture them? Who would deploy? One memory of that day was of the radio blaring out at full volume, tuned into the news, reporting on the House of Commons emergency debate on the Argentinian Invasion. Wherever the Falklands was, the British Government was not prepared to see them lost to Argentina without a fight. It was clear listening to the radio that morning that a negotiated settlement needed to be achieved by diplomatic means, or military force would have to be used to dislodge the Argentinian Forces and restore British sovereignty over the Falkland Islands. The immediate British response was to announce that a Task Force would be setting sail at once.

BELONGING TO 2 TROOP

In Aldershot, the next three weeks were marked by repeated parades and numerous reviews of kit and equipment. Montgomery Lines was a blizzard of activity as airborne units moved to full alert. Initially, 3 Troop was stood up for deployment as the Spearhead Troop.

Spearhead Troop was part of the Spearhead Battalion Group, identified to deploy world-wide on short notice to move. In April 1982, 3 Para was the Spearhead Battalion, with engineer support provided by 3 Troop. But with insufficient room on the SS Canberra, 3 Troop was subsequently stood down. Shortly after that decision was made, 2 Para was identified to reinforce 3 Commando Brigade. Their Commanding Officer made it clear that he wanted 'his troop', ie 2 Troop, to support him. We were heading South!

We understood that we would be obliged to move with what were euphemistically called 'light scales'. In simple terms, light scales meant no vehicles, so everything needed for any initial operations would have to be hauled on our backs. Consequently, as well as carrying spare clothing, rations, sleeping bag, water and ammunition, individual members of the Troop would have to also carry our share of any engineer tools, explosives, mine clearance equipment and engineer stores needed for the conflict ahead. What to take and what to leave behind were agonising questions. The answers would be dependent on a deployment plan that was yet to be agreed, let alone disseminated to those likely to be identified for the move to the South Atlantic. This resulted in a guessing game. What engineer challenges lay ahead? Would the Troop be faced with minefield clearance tasks? How could we help

CHAPTER 2

the infantry to live, move and fight? What distances would we expect to have to march and in what conditions? What was a reasonable weight each man might have to carry?

> As the days passed, plans became clearer. 3 Commando Brigade, along with the 3rd Battalion, The Parachute Regiment and 59 Independent Commando Squadron, Royal Engineers, set sail with Naval Task Force 317 between the 6th and the 9th of April. The Task Force included the aircraft carriers Hermes and Invincible, the guided missile destroyers Glamorgan, Sheffield, Coventry, Glasgow and Antrim and the frigates Brilliant, Plymouth and Arrow. Commanded by Admiral Fieldhouse from Northwood, it comprised a Carrier Battlegroup, an Amphibious Task Group, a South Georgia Task Group and a Sub-surface Task Group. On board the Amphibious Task Group was the Landing Force Task Group, (3 Commando Brigade). The Brigade Headquarters sailed on HMS Fearless, one of two Amphibious ships known as Landing Platform Dock (LPD), the other being HMS Intrepid, a ship 2 Troop was to become familiar with, as we shall see.

59 Independent Commando Squadron was the sister Squadron to 9 Parachute Squadron. Both units had demanding selection processes for acceptance of men from the Royal Engineers. In 59 Squadron's case, it was the All-Arms Commando course, a tough 5-week course at Commando Training Centre Lympstone preceded by a

rigorous 5-week 'beat-up' course to prepare individuals for the green beret course itself. Success meant earning the right to wear the green beret and a dagger emblem on their arm. For 9 Squadron, it was a preparatory fitness course called 'pre-para' followed by the Parachute Regiment's own fitness and endurance course known as 'P Company' and then a month-long Parachute training course (the Jumps Course) at RAF Brize Norton. All this earnt us the right to wear the coveted 'wings' badge on our uniform and the maroon beret. Unsurprisingly, each Squadron thought that their own selection course was the toughest and therefore their unit were the most prestigious.

Soon after the Task Force had set off, the decision was made to deploy a fifth battalion, 2nd Battalion, the Parachute Regiment, to bolster the strength of 3 Commando Brigade. Once that call had been made, it was always likely that 2 Troop would deploy with them. Two Troop was the Battalion's affiliated engineer troop and we had built up a strong relationship with them over many years. More recently, on a two-month training exercise in Kenya, the bond had grown stronger. As their Troop Commander, I knew all the officers in the Battalion, and the Troop Senior NCOs were well acquainted with the personalities in the Battalion Sergeants Mess. Lieutenant Colonel 'H' Jones, 2 Para's Commanding Officer appreciated his close support sapper Troop. Although he was notoriously sparing in his praise for good performance, he had recently written to Lieutenant Colonel Geoff Field, Commanding 36 Engineer Regiment, thanking 2 Troop for their contribution in Kenya. The close

CHAPTER 2

bond between the Troop and 2 Para extended still further, as many of the senior members of the troop lived on the same married quarters 'patch' in Aldershot as members of 2 Para and the Battalion and Squadron single soldiers' accommodation was in close proximity to each other.

Whilst the Troop was well recruited, a sensible decision was made by our new Officer Commanding, Chris Davies, to re-enforce us with an additional plant section and some heavy plant vehicles and equipment. So, our numbers swelled to 52, with the additional section, under the leadership of Corporal Bob Wilson, setting sail on the cargo ship, Europic Ferry. Bob was a diminutive figure, physically strong with a thoughtful disposition. He was a deeply knowledgeable and practical plant operator and a consistent, durable Junior NCO. The Troop was lucky to have him, and his section attached. They fitted in well.

2 Troop, 9 Parachute Squadron in Aldershot, February 1982.

BELONGING TO 2 TROOP

Capt Burns (9)

FROM LIEUTENANT COLONEL 'H' JONES OBE

2ND BATTALION
THE PARACHUTE REGIMENT
BRUNEVAL BARRACKS
ALDERSHOT
HAMPSHIRE GU11 2AZ

Aldershot Military) Ext
Aldershot 24431) 593

*9 PARA. SQN. R.E.
15 JAN 1982
A0306 A*

Lieutenant Colonel G W Field MBE
Commanding Officer
36 Engineer Regiment
Invicta Barracks
Maidstone
Kent

5 January 1982

Dear Geoff,

This is just a short note to say how very well Robbie Burns and 2 Troop did in Kenya. It really was a pleasure to have them with us, and we certainly would not have got half the value out of the exercise which we did without them. Thank you for letting them come with us.

Yours ever

H

CO : Geoff 10/1
OC 9 :
Capt Burns : Well done. It must have been a real chore.!!

A letter from Lieutenant Colonel 'H' Jones, CO 2 Para to Lieutenant Colonel Geoff Field, CO 36 Engineer Regiment, thanking 2 Troop for their efforts in Kenya in November and December 1981.

CHAPTER 2

The Band of the Parachute Regiment play at the quayside in Postsmouth as MV Norland casts off with 2 Para Group embarked. The 26th of April 1982.

Wives and girlfriends gathered at the quayside, Portsmouth to say goodbye to 2 Para Bn Group. Photo taken from the deck of the MV Norland.

MV Norland, heading South – April 1982.

SS Canberra. 2 Troop was helilifted onto Canberra 3 days before the landings at San Carlos.

CHAPTER 2

Lieutenant Colonels Hew Pike (3 Para) and 'H' Jones (2 Para), standing on the flight deck of SS Canberra at Ascension Island. 2 Troop sailed with 2 Para but cross-decked to support 3 Para for the invasion.

DIPLOMATIC NEGOTIATIONS

Even before the Argentinian invasion, on the 1st of April, the British diplomatic effort to secure a UN Security Council resolution had begun. Sir Anthony Parsons, our UN Ambassador had swung into action, summoning the Council to consider a resolution ordering the Argentinians to leave the Islands. Forty-eight hours later, after herculean efforts by Parsons, we had secured the two thirds majority needed amongst the 15 council members to secure UN Security Council Resolution 502, as drafted by the UK.

Chapter 3

EMBARKATION

Such was the culture in 9 Squadron at the time that when 2 Troop was identified for deployment, there was no shortage of volunteers to squeeze onto the ship with us. Before we sailed, there was time for a few days leave, and then the inevitable false starts before the transport finally arrived in Aldershot to move us and our kit to Portsmouth. The thoughtful and caring Families Officer, Captain Dick Barton arranged for a separate coach to take wives and girlfriends to the quayside for final farewells, making the embarkation unnecessarily emotional! Some of the single soldiers wondered what all the fuss was about! With the Band of the Parachute Regiment playing on the quayside, on the 26th of April, a grey, somewhat uninspiring day, MV Norland dropped lines and eased out of Portsmouth Harbour.

The Motor Vessel (MV) Norland was built in 1974 by AG Weser, in Bremerhaven, West Germany. She was 153 metres long, 25.2 metres wide and had a gross registered tonnage of 12,500 tons. Before being requisitioned by the Armed Forces, she was ploughing her trade on the Hull-Rotterdam ferry service. Her maximum capacity was 1244 passengers together with 520 cars. She had a complement of two full civilian crews to allow for shifts and leave, all based in Kingston-upon-Hull. There were also two Captains, Don Ellerby and Derek Wharton.

On the 17th of April, all hands from both crews were summoned to a meeting at 1030 in the morning at King George Dock, Hull. At the meeting, Don Ellerby announced that the Norland had been requisitioned by the military to support Operation Corporate, the British response to the Argentinian occupation of the Falklands Islands. This process had the rather unfortunate name of 'Ships Taken Up From Trade', with the acronym 'STUFT'. This arrangement supplemented the Royal Navy fleet in time of war. Merchant ships would be commanded by a small detachment of Royal Navy officers, operating through existing merchant navy chains of command. Volunteers were required to step forward to create a complement of navigators, catering staff, stewards and engineers from both crews to go South. By the end of the meeting, to their immense credit, a full complement of volunteers had stepped forward. At this time, the expectation was that the MV Norland would be employed moving military personal and equipment to Ascension Island, where they would be cross decked to Royal Navy vessels to complete the journey South into the war zone. This proved to be an overly optimistic assumption.

The next two days saw a flurry of activity at King George Dock, with a major refit of the MV Norland taking place at breakneck pace. Of the many items of equipment and stores bought on board, one vital item was hoisted onto the aft deck before her departure. One of the

CHAPTER 3

long-standing crew members and keen piano player, Roy (Wendy) Gibson had acquired a piano from the Flying Angel Mission to Seaman located near to the dock. Roy and his piano proved to be a huge morale booster for the troops as we sailed South. By the 21st of April, the MV Norland was ready to sail. Roy tickled the ivories and was accompanied by lots of singing as the North Sea ferry pulled through the locks, and departed Hull for the journey to Portsmouth, where their complement of soldiers from 2 Para Group were to embark.

Whist Captain Don Ellerby was appointed Master of the Ship, overall command was vested in Royal Navy Commander Christopher Esplin-Jones with his second in command, Lieutenant Commander Ian Hughes, supported by Naval Party 1850. Importantly for the civilian crew, all orders and instructions were channelled through the Master, who effectively remained in charge of the day-to-day running of the ship. The RN complement brought with it vital expertise in such activities as helicopter operations and anti-submarine avoidance techniques, areas not normally associated with a crossing of the North Sea to Rotterdam!

Once docked in Portsmouth harbour, much further work was needed to make Norland ready to join the Task Force. Extra fuel tanks were brought on board and a water desalination plant fitted with 11 rubber holding tanks strapped to one of the car decks. Two members of 2 Troop became very familiar with the workings of the desalination plant. Sapper Scottie Scott boarded ahead of the rest of the Troop to help construct the desalination plant. Sapper Billy Morris was 'volunteered' to look after this key equipment on the journey South. Billy was a Plant Operator mechanic by trade and well versed in both mechanical engineering and fluid dynamics, so he was the obvious choice to be tasked with managing this pivotal equipment. (Billy's epic story is covered later). Other major work included two steel plated helicopter decks welded to the superstructure whilst existing canteen and recreation areas were reconfigured for the journey ahead. Portsmouth also saw the embarkation of 2nd Battalion, The Parachute Regiment. The Battalion Group included 29 (Corunna) Battery, 4th Field Regiment, Royal Artillery, additional Royal Signals detachments and 2 Troop, 9 Parachute Squadron. With close to 1,000 soldiers of the 2 Para Group on board, we set sail.

Chapter 4

SAILING SOUTH

The initial journey South to Ascension Island, via Freetown, was a surreal experience for the Troop. To a large extent, isolated from the world outside, we could only speculate about the prospects of the Task Force heading into the South Atlantic, to enforce the newly advertised 200-mile total exclusion zone. The bulk of the Task Force, including our newly acquired parent sapper squadron, 59 Squadron, was assembling ahead of us at Ascension, so the Norland was in catch up mode. Committing to an amphibious landing on the Falkland Islands seemed a remote possibility during those early days on board. We were unsighted on the strategic and operational planning taking place on HMS Fearless, so had no feel for the likelihood or otherwise of a fight. Indeed, at this stage, I held on to the expectation that I would be available to attend my own wedding, planned for the 8th of May. The arrangements were finally cancelled only in the week before the event was due to take place. By way of amusement, the troop comedian, Lance Corporal Mick Humphries, arranged for numerous requests for wedding songs to be played on the ship's radio throughout the day of the 8th of May, just in case

'Troopie' had forgotten the significance of the date. The joke wore a bit thin after a while.

Our brief stop-over in Freetown, Sierra Leone, provided no respite for the Troop or the remainder of the complement on board. There was no shore leave and our intense training schedule continued, despite the tropical heat and humidity. Freetown had one connection with the Norland, albeit tenuous. Freetown was twinned with Kingston-upon-Hull through its association with the abolition of slavery in the early 1800s. The connection was William Wilberforce, Hull-born politician and emancipationist. (Freetown was established in 1792 for freed African-American, Afro-Caribbean and Liberated African slaves). Despite this connection, and in part because Freetown brought with it a terribly unpleasant odour, we were all pleased to lift anchor and continue on our journey to Ascension Island after less than 24 hours in the port.

In 1982, I was what was known as a 'second tour' troop commander. In other words, I had already served one tour of duty leading a troop before attending the Army's university, RMCS Shrivenham. Now coming to the end of my second stint of commanding at this level, I was due to be posted to Germany as a squadron second-in-command towards the end of the year. Being a Yorkshireman, I was fit, loved sport and was keen to impress. I remember receiving a posting order to join 9 Parachute Squadron after graduating in 1980 and thinking that there was no better job in the world. And so, it proved.

A more critical judge might conclude that I was inclined to subservience when dealing with the chain of command

CHAPTER 4

above me, a trait that would not necessarily benefit the Troop in the weeks ahead. Maybe that's too self-critical, but I was a touch shy, a little reticent and self-effacing and consequently took time to build professional relationships. As we sailed South on the MV Norland, I was most anxious that if my men were required to fight, I would be able to measure up and not let them down.

I shared a two-man cabin on the Norland with an old school mate, Jim Barry. Jim and I had attended Welbeck College, the Army's sixth form college together in 1974. Actually, Jim was in the year behind me, but in the same House (Harland), so I knew him well. He had been commissioned into the Royal Signals but found himself on attachment with 2 Para as an infantry Platoon Commander. This was not uncommon for junior officers in the Royal Signals as it gave them valuable insights into how the 'teeth arms' operated. Jim and I got on well. He was a kind and generous companion with a delightful sense of humour. In Kenya, 6 months previously, we had spent our R&R together on the coast near Mombasa after 5 weeks training at Nanuki in Northern Kenya and in the bush with 2 Para. To get to Mombasa, we caught the overnight rail service from Nairobi down to the coast. Travelling on a rickety old train but with first class service, it felt like a throw-back to colonial days with waiters, white linen and cocktails – a surreal experience. It was great fun and a world away from the MV Norland. Sadly, Jim was subsequently killed at Goose Green on the 28th of May.

The Troop's SNCOs, Staff Sergeant Pete Guerin and Sergeant Colin Sweeney were bunked up together with the battalion Senior NCOs, whilst the rest of the Troop were billeted tight together lower in the ship's quarterdeck. Pete was an experienced and trusted Staff Sergeant, older than the rest of the Troop and a steadying influence on the group, whilst Colin was a dynamic and unbelievably tough recce Sergeant. A high quality, amateur boxer in his younger days, he was light on his feet and moved across the ground quickly, even with a full pack on his back. Both men were instinctively loyal to 9 Parachute Squadron, loyal to their troop officer and loyal to their men. They set the tone for the rest of the Troop.

Our Plant section of 12 were separated from us on the Europic Ferry, and although we could view their vessel alongside the Norland in the convoy as it headed South, we were unable to communicate with each other for long stretches of the voyage. This proved immensely frustrating for Bob Wilson and his colleagues, out of the information loop and unaware of what was being planned.

One of the newer members of the Troop, Lance Corporal Derek Broadbent, was also embarked on the Europic Ferry. He was an experienced soldier and had recently earned his wings having been posted to 9 Squadron earlier in the year. Consequently, Derek was largely unknown to the rest of the Troop. A Plant Fitter by trade, Derek had also been trained on the new Clansman set of radios, and so was the obvious choice to drive the Troop Commander's land rover and operate the Clansman high frequency radio, the Cl 320. He remained on the Europic Ferry, isolated and unaware of what was happening, until the fleet dropped anchor at Ascension Island. He was then flown by helicopter to join

CHAPTER 4

the rest of the Troop on the Norland. So, for Derek, bonding with his new colleagues was both an essential and urgent necessity. (The Troop Commander's land rover remained afloat throughout the war.)

DIPLOMATIC NEGOTIATIONS CONCLUDE

Throughout April, and following UN resolution 502, a number of rounds of 'shuttle diplomacy' by US Secretary of State Al Haig took place. His aim was to find a diplomatic solution that would de-escalate the crisis. His attempts to find some common ground upon which to build a negotiated settlement involved a number of flights to London and Buenos Aires and then back to London. By the end of the month, he and his team had clocked up over 32,000 air miles. In Argentina, he was met with a weak government propped up by an overly confident military chiefs of staff dominated by the head of the Navy, Admiral Anaya. In London, he received an uncompromising position from Margaret Thatcher, but, confusingly, a more accommodating approach from Foreign Secretary Francis Pym. But by the 28th of April, Haig's final proposal to both countries to reach a diplomatic solution, (known as Haig Two) had been rejected by the Argentinian military junta, headed by General Galtieri. With the collapse of negotiations, Rear Admiral Sandy Woodward received a signal from the UK Joint Headquarters in Northwood...' 'In all respects, prepare for war by midnight April, the 29th.'

SOUTH GEORGIA SUCCESS

Good news was warmly received in the last week in April. Operation Paraquet, the operation to retake South Georgia, had been successful. The South Georgia Task Force, which had sailed ahead of the rest of the force, had included SBS, D Squadron SAS and M Company 42 Commando, and had taken the Argentinian surrender on the 25th of April. It had been a daring and at times chaotic adventure involving helicopters crash landing in blizzard conditions and an aborted first assault. But with HMS Antrim providing naval gunfire, at 2.45 that afternoon, a 75-man composite team landed by helicopter and closed in on Grytviken. Within 3 hours, the local commander, Captain Alfredo Astiz, had surrendered and the Union Jack was hoisted once more.

For those on board the Norland, this was welcome news indeed. But it also left us with the misleading impression that any future engagement on the Falklands was likely to meet little resistance and be equally successful. It was around this time that we learnt that the Maritime Exclusion Zone, a 200-mile zone around the Falkland Islands had now been declared a 'Total Exclusion Zone'

CHAPTER 4

meaning that enemy aircraft in the air and on the ground were now legitimate targets.

THE SINKING OF THE BELGRANO

A week later, there was news of more success. At 3pm on the 2nd of May, HMS Conqueror, one of three conventional submarines supporting the operation, had attacked the Argentine cruiser Belgrano. At 13,654 tons, Belgrano was one of only two capital ships in the Argentine Navy. She was 35 miles outside the Total Exclusion Zone when she was engaged. Two torpedoes struck the ship. Once out of range, Conqueror had upped periscope to see her listing heavily to port. With more than 1,000 men on board, the casualty list was likely to be high. She sank in heavy seas. Her two cruiser destroyer escorts left the scene without picking up survivors. It was later confirmed that 368 sailors lost their lives that afternoon.

The Belgrano's sinking left us with mixed emotions. My recollection is that we weren't too bothered about the issue of her being outside the Total Exclusion Zone. I think we all felt that if she was sailing near the Falklands, she was fair game. What bothered us to a degree was the heavy loss of life, and the growing realisation that we too were increasingly vulnerable, and a very long way from home. The South Atlantic Ocean is enormous and unrelenting. There is no respite from it. To be cast into lifeboats for over 24 hours as the weather turned into a full gale, as the crew of the Belgrano had endured, must have been terrifying. I recall that my second emotion was one of resolve. It was now becoming clear that we were in a conflict. This was not about military posturing whilst a diplomatic solution was to be found. There were to be no compromises. Our modest force with the most tenuous of logistical links back to Blighty had to succeed. And we were only going to get one crack at it.

The Troop's management team assembled on the 3rd of May with the Battalion's leadership team, to hear a presentation from the Principal Warfare Officer of one of the guided missile destroyers. (I can't recall which one). He had flown over to the MV Norland to brief us on the Task Force's weaponry and its ability to defend itself against Argentinian attack. The presentation was intended to be a morale boosting talk, aimed at building our confidence as we entered the Total Exclusion Zone. There was much talk about the effectiveness of the Royal Navy's radar and state of the art surface-to-air weapons, Sea Dart and Sea Wolf. No-one in the Troop missed the sad irony when news of HMS Sheffield's demise, following a direct hit from an air launched Exocet missile, was announced the next day.

HMS SHEFFIELD

HMS Sheffield was a Type 42 guided missile destroyer launched in 1971. She was equipped with Sea Dart and was positioned East of the

CHAPTER 4

convoy on the morning of the 4th of May. Her task was to provide early warning of any Argentinian air or naval attack. She was struck by an Exocet missile amidships around 10am, It had been launched from an Argentinian Super Etendard aircraft flying low level from about 20 miles to her West. Twenty-one members of her crew were killed that morning and the ship had to be abandoned. She was reboarded on the 9th of May and taken into tow by HMS Yarmouth, but sank the next day, the 10th of May.

It was then that things started to get very serious indeed. The Troop, along with the rest of the Battalion, began to take rather more interest in visiting our wonderful Regimental Padre, the Rev David Cooper. The queue outside his little office on board was getting longer. For some, they wanted some spiritual guidance, whilst others were seeking the ultimate insurance policy of having their God on their side.

David was much more than an Army Chaplain. He was also an Army Champion shot at Bisley, home of the National Rifle Association. As a consequence, he used these skills to help prepare the Battalion's snipers. The Sniper Platoon assembled for target practice off the stern of MV Norland on most days as we sailed South, coached by the best shot on board, the Padre. He was later to be Mentioned in Dispatches for his courage during the Battle for Goose Green.

Chapter 5

ASCENSION ISLAND

Ascension Island lies 4,000 miles from England and almost 4,000 miles from the Falklands. It is a small volcanic Island in the middle of the Atlantic Ocean, halfway between Brazil and Africa. The only vegetation on the Island is the tropical rain forest on the summit and upper slopes of the aptly named Green Mountain. A deep Atlantic swell makes landing by conventional landing craft impractical except in the small cove of English Bay. There is no port on the Island so supplies have to be cross decked from ships anchored at sea onto smaller vessels that can access English Bay.

Ascension has an impressive airfield called 'Wideawake', with a 11,000 foot long runway. Trans-Atlantic aircraft can land and take off here. This became, for a short time in 1982, the busiest runway in the world.

Substantial elements of the Task Force had already congregated at Ascension Island and dropped anchor by the time it came into view. MV Norland was one of the last ships to heave to, finally dropping anchor on the 7th of May. The rest of the Task Force had been conducting amphibious and helicopter drills, and re-stowing stores and equipment whilst they waited for our arrival. The first elements of the Task Force had been loitering at Ascension for nearly three weeks, re-organising supplies and equipment. 3 Para, embarked on SS Canberra, arrived alongside Ascension on the 19th of April and remained there for 17 days. Their preparation for the future land battle included a ten-mile tab (march) across the island and weapon live firing for all their small arms and support weapons, including mortars and anti-tank weapons. By the time we arrived at Ascension, SS Canberra had set off South. But for 2 Para Group, we only had a pause of less than 24 hours before continuing our voyage South as part of the Task Force.

At Ascension, close to the equator, it was hot. The Troop did not get the chance to disembark and stretch our legs. Assembled at anchor were about 20 ships, including HMS Fearless, 5 of the six Landing Ships Logistic (LSLs), a number of frigates, the roll on-roll off ferry Elk, Europic Ferry and various refuellers. Other elements of the Task Force including the Carrier Battle Group and the South Georgia Battle Group were already deep in the South Atlantic – when we arrived, but it still looked like an impressive gathering to us.

Whilst at anchor, the lads were cooped up on board whilst I flew off to meet my new boss, Major Roddy Macdonald. Roddy and his Squadron Headquarters team on RFA Sir Tristram, anchored nearby. Roddy was also

CHAPTER 5

part of 3 Commando Brigade's 'R' Group, and a key advisor to Brigadier Thompson on Engineer matters. As such, he would normally have been found on HMS Fearless with his Brigade Headquarters colleagues. But the rest of his Squadron were based on the Sir Tristram, the agreed RV for our meeting.

Concerned about the relationship that needed to be forged, and hungry for information about the engineer's likely role, I was keen to meet my new colleagues and brethren from 59. Although I had met Roddy briefly before joining 9 Squadron, I had not served with him before. He was tall, athletic and a top-class hang glider pilot. In many ways an unconventional leader, he was a deep thinker, not bound by convention and able to work from first principles. Articulate and confident, he had strong views about how sappers could best be deployed in war. I now know that he made significant contributions to the overall plan for the land battle, and helped quash some of the less tactically sound proposals being proposed by the Task Force, including one plan being championed by the Royal Navy to construct a runway on West Falkland. The idea was to deploy the RAF and Royal Navy Harrier Force ashore, gain air superiority and then conduct an amphibious landing onto East Falkland. As Roddy pointed out, the Task Force was in no position to sustain offensive operations for the many weeks it would have taken to build such significant infrastructure on West Falkland.

There were some connections which were to make my relationship with my new functional master easier than it might have been. Firstly, I had served with 59 Independent

Commando Squadron before my degree course and had earned the right to wear a green beret as well as a maroon one. So, I was part of their 'club'. Next, the Squadron Second-in-Command, Dave Chipp, was also a Welbexian and good friend, as was fellow troop commander, Bob Hendicott, who commanded 1 Troop. Bob and I were later to command the same regiment, 36 Engineer Regiment in the early 1990s too.

Thirdly, and most importantly, from the outset, my new boss, Roddy Macdonald was intent on being supportive and welcoming. This was to prove crucially important as the campaign progressed. At the time, I felt that this sense of being valued and being part of the team was not understood by some in the teeth arms we supported. Or maybe they just didn't care that much. But Roddy cared, and that was a big deal for an independent troop commander.

What became apparent was that this mutual respect fostered at officer level did not necessarily translate at SNCO level and amongst the other ranks. Perhaps this was not surprising, partly because they only interacted occasionally and not in any formal way. Also, both organisations were deeply competitive about the part they were to play in the campaign. Inevitably, 2 Troop would be at a disadvantage in that respect, as we were now part of a very different team, and the men felt that keenly.

Chapter 6

INTO THE SOUTH ATLANTIC

Having arrived at Ascension on the morning of the 7th of May, the MV Norland weighed anchor and set off into the South Atlantic at 2200 hours that evening. For 2 Troop, the mood changed as the prospect of engaging with the enemy increased. Training on board the MV Norland picked up pace. Every nook and cranny were used to conduct medical training, map reading practice, weapons training and specialist mine identification and clearance training. PT involved marching along gangways and up and down ladders with and without kit. Troop training was led by the three able Section Corporals, John (Jock) Ferry, Scott Wilson, and Kev Cowling. Each was knowledgeable, committed and professional. Each wanted to ensure that everyone was as ready as they could possibly be for any future possibility. Under their guidance, the Troop came together and became fiercely loyal and independent.

Jock and Scott were established 9 Squadron Junior NCOs. They had worked together for some time and were firm friends. Although very different in character, they complemented each other well. Scott was fit, athletic, focused and confident. He was a big character with a great sense of humour and was liked and admired by the entire Troop. Consequently, he was the litmus test of the guys' morale and well-being. He had recently married Jean, whose sister was also married to an NCO in 3 Para, so the Wilson family was fully committed to Army life.

On first meeting, Jock came across as a dour Scot, but he had a rich, understated sense of humour. Twenty-seven years old in 1982, he had been married to Sandra for 4 years and had a young baby (Gavin), born only three months before they set sail. He was the strongest combat engineer in the Troop. He was also an expert trainer as well as leader of his section. Both Jock and Scott were massively proud of their 9 Squadron roots. So close were they that Jock subsequently named his second son after Scott, in his memory.

Things were much harder for Kev Cowling, newly posted in from the Royal Engineers Training Regiment and not yet fully accepted into the Troop. He had something to prove and would need to adapt his leadership style to win over some of the more experienced sappers in the Troop. As he began to realise on the journey South, just shouting orders was never going to cut it in this close-knit community.

Medical training took on renewed focus. One new procedure that was being adopted, was the carriage and use of saline drips by front line soldiers, not just medical orderlies. Practising for the use of such drips in the event of casualties through artillery shrapnel or gunshot wounds was essential. They were administered through the rectum, and so section and troop level

CHAPTER 6

training in their use was the cause of some amusement. Volunteers were needed for the practical demonstration. When none stepped forward, I was volunteered, much to the mirth and enjoyment of all. Luckily, no one had a camera at the time!

Heavier seas and colder air marked our gradual, ominous, relentless journey South. I remember it as a gradual, dawning realisation that the MV Norland was unlikely to turn around and head back North. Preparations for a possible air attack galvanised the Troop, with drills for 'action stations' now being taken seriously. Ironically, as instructed by the ship's naval detachment, the first action for embarked troops when coming under air attack was to don helmets and lie on our bunks. In some cases, these bunks were positioned at exactly the height above sea level where an enemy Exocet missile would strike the ship.

Meanwhile, difficult questions were being asked about the overall plan for the land battle ahead and our part in it. Increasing interest was being taken in the robustness of casualty evacuation plans. More blue airmail letters were being written home. It didn't cross anyone's mind that these letters weren't going anywhere any time soon. They were just stored on board! The absence of information available about the Falkland Islands, the lack of quality maps and the lack of any intelligence on the enemy's whereabouts were all beginning to creep into centre stage in people's minds.

Unbeknown to the Troop, the decision to land 3 Commando Brigade at San Carlos water was finally taken by Brigadier Julian Thompson, Commander 3 Commando Brigade, on the 10th of May in the conference room on HMS Fearless. On MV Norland, we were unaware that a number of options for the forthcoming land assault had been actively considered, including a landing on West Falkland, and landings much nearer to Port Stanley. But it was felt that Falkland Sound offered some limited protection against low level enemy aircraft, and the landing sites were sufficiently far from known enemy defensive positions to allow time to establish 3 Commando Brigade ashore.

PEBBLE ISLAND

On the night of the 14th of May, 45 men from D Squadron SAS supported by a Naval Gunfire Support team from 148 Battery, 29 Commando, attacked the Argentinian held airfield on Pebble Island, North of West Falkland. They landed by Sea King helicopter in fierce winds and used demolition charges to destroy 11 aircraft without losing a man.

The Pebble Island attack was reported the next day on the Norland and gave us all renewed hope. Its success was evidence of what a well-handled British force could achieve against far larger numbers of the Argentinians.

The Troop's last few days on MV Norland were notable for intensive briefings, rough sea conditions, grey skies, and repeated calls to 'Action Stations'. We caught up

CHAPTER 6

with the Canberra on the 11th of May, the same day as the Pebble Island assault, and it was around this time that we first got details of the plan for the amphibious landings. By the 13th of May, the convoy was 1,000 miles East of Buenos Aries and by the 15th of May, we were just 280 miles from the Falklands. It was then that I cross decked by helicopter to LSL Sir Tristram, to receive my engineer briefing from Roddy Macdonald and his Squadron Headquarters team and then produced troop orders for the next day. Our role was to support 2 Para, who were to land at San Carlos, a small settlement on East Falkland. We expected to be in the first wave ashore and our initial role was to check and clear the beach area for possible land mines.

Chapter 7

A CHANGE OF PLAN

Three days later, on the 18th of May, my and 2 Troop's war was to change dramatically. With 5 battalions or Commandos (the Royal Marine equivalent of a battalion) and only four engineer troops in the Task Force, it was decided that 2 Troop would be moved to support the 3rd Battalion, The Parachute Regiment (3 Para), currently embarked on SS Canberra, not 2 Para. This was unwelcome news for the Troop. We had worked hard for the past two years to build up close relations with 2 Para. Not only were we now going to war without our parent squadron alongside, but also without our affiliated infantry battalion. With little ceremony and even less preparation, the Troop assembled on the rear helicopter deck of MV Norland awaiting three Sea King helicopter lifts onto SS Canberra. I was concerned, not least about our kit. We had personal weapons and webbing with us, and our bergans with engineer small stores, sleeping bag, spare clothing, rations and water. But we also needed to make sure our 'follow-on kit, moved with us too. Each of us had a sausage bag with other personal clothing and kit we hoped to see again at some stage in the campaign. Our G1098 stores, boxed and stored on the MV Norland, had many of the specialist tools and equipment we might need ashore. But it was made clear to us that we had to move across to the Canberra with weapons, webbing and our bergans only. So impossibly difficult choices had to be made to identify what we could cram into already bulging rucksacks, and what would have to be left behind. We were not to know then that we didn't see the bulk of our engineer equipment and stores that were left on the MV Norland until the conflict had concluded.

With our kit packed and a few brief farewells to our 2 Para chums, we assembled on the upper stern deck next to the improvised helipad awaiting our Sea King lifts. In heavy South Atlantic seas, we were then plucked off the Norland and dumped onto the deck of the Canberra, known as 'the great white whale'.

For 2 Troop, the MV Norland had become our home for over three weeks. Once cross-decked onto the Canberra, that connection, that sense of belonging, both to 2 Para Group and to the ship that looked after us as we ploughed through the South Atlantic, was lost. We knew very few people on our new floating home. The ship was bursting with soldiers from three battalions and their supporting arms. We newly arrived sappers had to find our own accommodation. The men bedded down in corridors as all bunks were taken.

There wasn't much of a welcoming party. Lance Corporal Paul (Ginge) Moore remembers that his section shared accommodation with Naval Party 8901, the Royal Marine detachment who had responsibility for the Falkland Islands. My sappers were not made welcome and

CHAPTER 7

were denied access to the Marines' showers and toilets or 'heads'. All in all, the atmosphere wasn't pleasant. Taff Sweeney remembers that even as a Sergeant, he had to find a corner of a corridor to sleep. There was no offer of a shared bunk. A couple of days later, he had to fight his way in to be present at the CO's O Group.

What motivates people to fight is not just about Queen and Country. We wanted to feel needed: part of a team. We wanted to feel that those around us cared for us and valued us. To ask us to fight, and to fight hard, we needed to feel that risking our lives was worth it and that the alternative would be unacceptable to comrades and friends. For 2 Troop, those motivations had been removed at a stroke, and it was going to be extremely challenging to rebuild that spirit in the time we had left. We could and did generate that camaraderie amongst ourselves but felt very little connection with the wider battalion team

Morale took a dive. Lots of questions were being asked. Who were 3 Para? What was the Commanding Officer, Lieutenant Colonel Hew Pike, like? What was our role to be? How would our new infantry masters use their engineers? What was expected of 2 Troop? How did we get our rations, our ammunition, our engineer stores? Did the Battalion have any assault pioneers? Did they take engineers seriously? Lots of questions with not many answers.

Over the next 2 days, as well as preparing for the forthcoming landings, the Troop attempted to build some new relationships. Our new Commanding Officer, Lieutenant Colonel Hew Pike, was charming and took time to talk to the whole troop the next day. We assembled as a Troop on one of the lower decks and he quietly talked to us about the likely tasks ahead. Hew Pike had joined 3 Para as a young platoon commander in 1963, had been Adjutant of 1 Para, commanded A Company, 3 Para as a Major and had also been Brigade Major, 16 Parachute Brigade, so he was Parachute Regiment through and through. As such, he had got to know 9 Squadron and knew our capabilities. He was a supporter and was supportive. I think he recognised the predicament we were in and the challenges we faced.

Support and guidance also came in the form of Patrols Company Commander, Major Pat Butler. Pat was known to the Troop, having previously commanded P Company as the senior instructor, a course that members of the Troop had attended before joining the Squadron. Pat recognised that the Troop needed a friend. He was patient, generous and showed excellent leadership in making us feel welcome.

Chapter 8
THE LANDINGS AT PORT SAN CARLOS

With only 24 hours to the amphibious landing in San Carlos Bay, the Troop faced further disruption. By all accounts, concern was expressed back in London that the Canberra was a vulnerable target for Argentinian attack, and with three battalion groups squeezed on board, her loss would have been catastrophic. So, a decision was taken to cross deck one of the battalion groups onto HMS Intrepid, one of the two amphibious warfare ships in the fleet. Intrepid had a Landing Platform Dock (LPD) which allowed landing craft to be floated inside her hull.

3 Para Group was selected to transfer onto Intrepid. This time, the Troop moved by Landing Craft Utility, (LCU), in heavy seas, and squeezed onto HMS Intrepid ready for the run in to San Carlos. The short journey across a rough stretch of open water felt risky. Harrier aircraft were flying above us and landing and taking off from one of the two carrier ships close by. An Argentinian air attack during this troop re-organisation would have been catastrophic.

BELONGING TO 2 TROOP

On board HMS Intrepid, there was even less room than on the SS Canberra, so our final night at sea was spent in the only spare space available, the small naval chapel. It was a modest room capable of holding a service for about 30 people. Almost all of the 40 men from 2 Troop were crammed onto the floor, although a couple of guys showed some enterprise and opened a glass display case. Gently moving the religious artefacts that were on display to one side, they slept in the display cabinet itself.

OPERATION SUTTON

D-day for Operation Sutton, the landings on East Falklands, was the 21st of May. H-Hour was 210639z May 82. The landings were supported by a diversionary attack by D Squadron, SAS onto Argentinian positions at Darwin, South of the landing area, and by naval gunfire from HMS Glamorgan onto Berkeley Sound, to the North-East, one of the sites considered for the main landings and then rejected. The first troops of the main landing force waded ashore below San Carlos settlement a few minutes before 4am (local) on that Friday morning. 2 Para had been late embarking on their LCUs from MV Norland, but moved through the settlement to climb up to the summit of Sussex Mountain. 40 Commando followed and secured the settlement. At this stage, as

CHAPTER 8

daylight broke, no Argentinian air attacks had been launched.

On HMS Intrepid, we briefly tried to sleep on the night of the 20th of May. In truth, I doubt any of us actually slept at all. The Troop was to support the 3 Para landings onto what was known as Green Beach at Port San Carlos. We were in the second wave of the landings, with 40 Commando and 2 Para in the first wave onto San Carlos, (as opposed to Port San Carlos, the next bay North). After a middle of the night reveille, we packed up, strapped our kit on, prepared our weapons and mustered for the queue to the floating dock on HMS Intrepid.

Members of 2 Troop prepare to be cross decked from the MV Norland onto SS Canberra. Pictured are Derek Broadbent, Kev Lillicrap, Taff Sweeney, Pete Guerin, John Hare and Scott Wilson.

BELONGING TO 2 TROOP

HMS Intrepid. 2 Troop went ashore from Intrepid, via LCVP.

2 Troop about to go ashore at Port San Carlos.

CHAPTER 8

Soup being served to members of 3 Para on the 21st of May. A whale jaw stands behind the group at Port San Carlos settlement.

Troop headquarters trench at Port San Carlos.

Tea being offered to Willy Macdonald by the residents of Port San Carlos settlement.

Staff Sergeant Pete Guerin digging in.

CHAPTER 8

Corporal Jock Ferry in reflective mood.

On guard duty during one of the many air attacks.

As we queued in the darkness deep in the bowels of HMS Intrepid, there were long periods of inactivity interspersed with some short periods of frantic action. It wasn't total darkness, as gangways were lit with low voltage red lights that gave us a small sense of perspective. We stood in orderly lines whilst belted ammunition, hand grenades and other pieces of ordnance were distributed to each of us, adding to the burden each man had to carry. With cam cream on, weapons and radios checked, final instructions were given. Then, inevitably, there was confusion whilst men and equipment were loaded onto each landing craft. Standing, waiting in the semi-darkness, anxiety was written onto every face. For many, these were reflective moments despite the hustle and bustle. Would we be unopposed? Would there be enemy air attacks? Would the beach be mined? As daybreak arrived, we wondered whether we were behind schedule? (We were!) It was billed as a night amphibius approach, but delays led to the Troop embarking on our landing craft just as the sun began to rise. As Mick Humphries succinctly put it, 'They've cocked that up!'

One bit of good news was that the Commanding Officer, Lieutenant Colonel Hew Pike, boarded 2 Troop's landing craft as we had the unenviable task of clearing the beachhead of any enemy mines ahead of the main body of the Battalion. Somehow, his presence provided some level of surety. The boss was on board with us. But as the landing craft approached the beach, a significant fire fight was taking place to our left on a prominent feature called Fanning Head. We had little understanding then of what was happening, but it was enough to remind us that this

CHAPTER 8

was to be no picnic, as Brigadier Julian Thompson would later observe.

As we approached the beach itself, what should have been a heroic assault landing turned into a bit of a farce. Our landing craft had been edging forward, with a crew member on the bow prodding the mirky water with a long pole to try to gauge the depth ahead. With 100 metres to go, the vessel came to a shuddering halt. We had run aground. Accompanied by the sound of machine gun fire on the adjacent hillside, we stood and waited. Eventually a smaller landing craft was brought alongside, and we all leapt, one by one across onto the alternative transport which proceeded to chug the last few metres to the beach. It was all pretty undignified, but we were ashore!

Events that morning have become a blur in people's minds. There were, thankfully, no mines on the beach and landing area. So, the Troop's sections detailed to clear the beaches had an easy time of it. And there were no air attacks as the landings took place. We were lucky, very lucky! But an Argentinian force of about 40 soldiers were seen hightailing it out of San Carlos settlement up the higher ground to the East. We later discovered that they had been sleeping in the woolsheds at the settlement that night, having recovered from Fanning Head. The Troop witnessed the tragedy that then unfolded. Unwittingly, a Sea King helicopter with an underslung load eased forward of the Battalion over the settlement in direct view of the retreating enemy. It was accompanied by two Gazelle escort helicopters. The Sea King realised it was in danger, ditched its load and quickly scooted below the horizon. Both gazelles were engaged with small arms fire and crashed into the sea alongside the settlement. To everyone's disgust and anger, the Argentinians continued to engage the crew as they struggled in the water. Three of the four men were killed. The fourth was badly wounded. It was a rude awakening for the Troop. We had a clear view during the attack but could do nothing to stop it.

At some stage that morning, we located a reasonable site within the Battalion perimeter to make our own and began digging-in to the West of the settlement around some gorse bushes. We were not allocated a defensive position by the Battalion. I just got on and chose one. By then, the first of many air raid warnings was heard, and the first of many Argentinian air sorties was seen overhead.

The first aircraft to appear that morning were two Pucara ground attack aircraft. We could hear them but couldn't really see this first action. Both aircraft were brought down, one by handheld Stinger anti-aircraft missile fired by an SAS party recovering from Sussex Mountain. The second was brought down by one of the ships in San Carlos Sound. Our first sighting was an Aeromacchi to our West, flying low over Fanning Head and targeting what I now know as the Leander class frigate, HMS Argonaut. At the time, I had no idea what type of aircraft it was. We could identify Pucaras, Skyhawks and Mirages, but not this thing. A barrage of anti-aircraft fire didn't prevent it getting four rockets way, but all failed to hit their target.

Sometime later that morning, the Argentinian Airforce arrived in earnest. Wave after wave of attack came in at

CHAPTER 8

very low level. They were looking to inflict maximum damage on the fleet, all at anchor or milling around in the Sound. Aircraft were mainly Mirages or Skyhawks. We were largely spectators although there were some vain attempts to join the fight with our SLRs and in one case, an SMG. HMS Antrim was hit and crippled by bombs and rockets. Whilst our old friend the Norland narrowly avoided being hit by two 1000lb bombs with spouts of water erupting around her. I was not alone in watching and praying for her and her crew. HMS Brilliant was then hit by Mirages, coming in at suicidally low level to avoid detection and engagement by Sea Dart.

The air battle raged for the best part of six hours as we dug in and watched. First, we would hear and see a Mirage, or a Skyhawk come in fast and low over the surrounding isthmus, then it would be followed by a Harrier, quickly launching its air-to-air missiles. If the enemy aircraft got away its bombs, it was only a matter of luck whether it missed its target or not. In a number of cases that morning, the outcome was a kill for the Harrier. It escaped none of us that this was a battle we had to win. If our capital ships suffered major damage, we would be in deep trouble. Without the likes of MV Norland, SS Canberra, HMS Fearless or Intrepid, the land force would be marooned and with no chance of winning any land conflict.

I learned later that evening in the first of the Battalion 'O' groups that the Argentines had lost 16 aircraft, a daily casualty rate it could not sustain.

Chapter 9

THE FIRST WEEK ASHORE

The Troop's first week ashore was notable for a number of different reasons. Everyone was relieved to be on the ground. We felt in control of our circumstances and able to manage the risks, whereas on board ship, we were reliant on others for protection. Digging in was comforting but the ground conditions were wet. Nights standing in trenches a foot deep in cold water were not too much fun. Initially, we had no large packs as we had come ashore wearing only 'fighting order' which consisted of webbing, ammunition, two days rations, engineer hand tools and limited amounts of explosives. It was a big morale booster some 3 days later to be re-united with our personal large packs. They had, at last, been heli-lifted ashore. Our last day before the arrival of our bergans was a day surviving on powdered soup and cups of tea. We now had our sleeping bags, even if we couldn't use them because our trenches were waterlogged!

On a couple of occasions in that first week, a huge steel pot of soup appeared, accompanied by the Port San Carlos farmer's wife. She trekked round each of the trenches which now surrounded the farmstead and ladled out the steaming broth to each of those on guard. It was very well received by all. Each day was concluded with a battalion briefing session in the Port San Carlos farmhouse itself. I joined the Battalion O Group, and would hear of the latest count in the air/sea battle in 'bomb alley' as it became known. Typically, 6 to 8 enemy aircraft were reported as shot down each day by either ground to air missile, (Rapier) or by Harrier. Everyone was acutely aware that the enemy attacks on our shipping could, if successful, change the balance in favour of the Argentinians. But increasingly, the air battle began to feel like a battle we would win.

The Troop had a ringside seat, watching each air attack by the Argentinian Air Force and each air-to-air battle when Harriers followed them into San Carlos Bay. Cheers rang out across the Troop when a Mirage, Skyhawk or Super-Etendard aircraft went down. By the end of the week, it was clear that the Argentinians could not sustain such losses each day. Mick Humphries recalled one air attack that week, which triggered a nearby Rapier missile launch. Unfortunately, the anti-aircraft weapon's system was faulty, and the missile cartwheeled down the hillside, towards the Troop defensive position. Staff Sergeant Pete Guerin had to dive out of the way to avoid it, causing much amusement amongst the rest of the Troop. A subsequent attack by an Argentinian Pucara aircraft on the Troop position resulted in a mad scramble for cover, as its machine guns strafed our newly dug trenches.

CHAPTER 9

HMS ANTELOPE

On D+3, Sunday the 23rd of May, amid repeated Argentinian air attacks on the fleet in Falkland Sound, HMS Antelope was hit by two 1000lb bombs delivered by enemy Skyhawks. One penetrated aft on the Starboard side, the second struck below the bridge on the port side, killing a steward and injuring two others in the Petty Officers Mess. Neither bomb detonated. That afternoon, Sergeant Prescot and Warrant Officer Phillips, both Royal Engineer bomb disposal experts, attempted to deal with the two bombs whilst the crew were evacuated to the fo'c'sle. They were dealing with the first bomb when it exploded, killing Prescot and badly injuring Phillips. The remaining crew were evacuated that evening. Soon after, the anchorage was shaken by a series of explosions in the ship's magazines. Antelope broke into two and sank the next day.

We all remember the enormous flash of light and the explosions on the Sunday evening. HMS Antelope was in clear sight and so we knew she was in trouble after the air raid that lunchtime. As darkness fell, we lost sight of her, but it took little imagination to work out that she had perished that night. Little did we know at the time that two of our own Royal Engineers cap badge were on board trying to save her at the time.

One early task on arrival at Port San Carlos was to clear the local community centre of any booby traps left by the recently departed Argentinian detachment. As it happened, they had left in haste, and had not had the time or the inclination to set any traps. But, once the building had been cleared, lots of contraband was discovered, including a Naval flag and cigarettes, both stolen by the Argentinians from the Moody Brook Royal Marine barracks in the previous weeks. Our heroes from 2 Troop nobly recovered these items, clearly intending to return them to their rightful owners at the end of the conflict!

At this point, it felt to the Troop that the engineer effort was inconsistent and haphazard. Key stores began to arrive ashore by mexi-float. Scott Wilson, Ginge Moore and others built a water point for the Battalion, and the entire Troop was engaged in building our first ever Harrier landing pad. To assist with this task, a QMSI, (Quartermaster Sergeant Instructor) from 38 Engineer Regiment was brought ashore together with his leather briefcase, much to the Troop's amusement. Unaccustomed to living in the field, our new arrival was paired up with Sergeant Taff Sweeney. Taff made sure that our guest was fed and watered and helped him settle into the Troop HQ trench. Equally, our guest quickly reminded Jock Ferry of the basics of Harrier pad construction, and our sappers soon adapted to the art of 'kicking tin'.

But two things frustrated the Troop. Firstly, Royal Marines who were digging in nearby were pinching the metal planking, which was vital to completing the pad, and were using it to construct their trenches. Secondly,

CHAPTER 9

the pad wasn't used and was eventually stripped out in order to make way for the full runway. Unbeknown to us, this runway became a turning point in the war. Once Harrier jets could operate from land, they had excellent loiter capability and could defend the landing area and the nearby capital ships from enemy air attack.

In the first few days ashore, we also provided engineer support to Battalion fighting patrols which operated each night beyond the perimeter of the Battalion defensive positions. One patrol, which included Lance Corporals John Hare and Ginge Hall from the Troop, went badly wrong with disastrous consequences.

Chapter 10

BLUE ON BLUE[1]

The Argentinian unit on Fanning Head was still concerning Lieutenant Colonel Hew Pike. A unit, known as Combat Team Eagle, was nicknamed the Fanning Head Mob (FHM) at Brigade Headquarters. We now know that it was commanded by 2nd Lieutenant Roberto Oscar Reyes and consisted of a detachment of 20 men, two 81mm mortars, and a pair of 105mm recoilless rifles. This detachment had set up an Observation Post (OP) on Fanning Head, having been flown across from Goose Green on the 14th of May. An attempt to deal with the Fanning Head Mob by 3 Special Boat Service on the morning of the 21st of May had only achieved partial success, with 2nd Lt Reyes and elements of his OP team still on the headland as we went ashore later that day. This was the firefight the Troop could see and hear as they landed on Green Beach 2.

Consequently, on the second night ashore Jock Ferry and Ginge Moore, accompanied a battalion fighting patrol. Its mission was to destroy Reyes' cache of Argentinian weapons and equipment, thought to have been secreted to

---

(1) Abridged from 'Friendly Fire in the Falklands' by Dr AD Chissel.

the North of the headland. After a briefing, they deployed by Rigid Raider round the headland and then spent a cold, wet night searching the area. Around daybreak, they located 2 Wombat type anti-tank guns, several mortar tubes and a Cymbeline mortar locating radar, half buried in the gorse. John Ferry takes up the story,

> 'Instead of using our explosives that we carried in our Bergans overnight, I decided to use the Argie's own ammunition... I then blew up two of the Argie Wombats and other stores and associated ammunition. I overcooked the amount of explosive packed around the guns and the portable ground radar, because when I set off the charges, myself and Ginge Moore were only about 150m away and bits were flying bloody everywhere.'

On his return to the 2 Troop defensive position, Jock heard that his Section second-in-command had now been tasked to join a further 3 Para patrol. That night, Lance Corporals John Hare and Ginge Hall supported a second fighting patrol under similar orders, with disastrous consequences.

Earlier that afternoon, Major David Collett, Officer Commanding A Company, 3 Para, gave orders for a fighting patrol based mainly on a section from 3 Platoon. It was a clearing patrol, as 2nd Lieutenant Reyes' FHM were still thought to be in the vicinity. There was also a requirement to investigate reports of a further ammunition dump in the Findlay Rocks area with a view to blowing it up. John Hare had already spent the afternoon on Settlement Rocks

CHAPTER 10

helping dig in elements of the battalion, but was nominated, along with Ginge Hall, to provide sapper support for the fighting patrol. John remembers handing over his Light Machine Gun magazines and clearing his pouches of field dressings, to make way for explosives and detonators. In addition, twenty-five metres of detonator cord was wrapped round his body in preparation for the night ahead.

John Hare's understanding from the pre-patrol briefing was that no other patrols were operating that night – it became apparent the next morning that this was not the case. Without a battalion patrols radio net and without a co-ordinated battalion patrols programme, the company level patrols were unsighted on other 'friendly force' activities that night.

The A Company patrol moved out after dusk, heading North through a D Company screen, in cold and miserable weather conditions. One of the Patrol later recalled that it was the coldest night he could ever remember. An early encounter with a herd of wild horses unsettled the patrol, and despite repeated stops throughout the night, no enemy and no ammunition dump were located by daybreak on Sunday the 23rd.

As light improved, the group found themselves on the forward slope to one side of a re-entrant called Fisherman's Valley. As they got their bearings, they spotted a platoon-sized body of soldiers about 800 metres away, coming over the crest of the opposite valley. The patrol paused, trying to identify the men across the valley. Their two (machine) gun-groups took up position whilst the riflemen attempted to scramble back into dead ground. As they crawled across the heather to a better position, they were raked by machine gun fire from across the valley. John Hare takes up the story.

> 'It was while we were here that silhouettes, lots of them, became visible across the valley about 800-900 metres away. Word went around that there was enemy (to our) front. The plan was (that) the GPMGs would move over to some better cover and the remainder of the patrol would move back up the incline and get into dead ground. As soon as we began to crawl up the slope, the day lit up with the sound of machine gun fire. I was hit almost immediately. Lance Corporal Hall was beside me. Bullets were pocking the ground all around us. I pressed my face deep into the ground bracing myself for the next bullet to strike and prayed.'

Machine gun fire from C Company chased the patrol as they attempted to find cover over the hill. At this stage, 6 of the 14 patrol members had received bullet wounds. Whilst under fire, the patrol commander ordered his radio operator to call in mortar fire on the 'enemy' position. But it appears that, in the confusion, grid co-ordinates provided to A Company Headquarters may have been those of the A Company patrol position, not the location of the group of soldiers who they assumed were enemy infantry. Unfortunately, similar grid co-ordinates were also sent by radio by the C Company patrol engaged in the fire fight, so re-enforcing the view that an Argentinian

CHAPTER 10

unit was in the A Company patrol's location. In any event, the A Company patrol now faced a barrage of mortar and artillery fire. Lance Corporal John Hare again...

> 'During the crawl, the first artillery rounds came in. It was (a) sickening sound, then silence, then bang. As the artillery bounded through us, we followed it up the hill eventually getting into some dead ground and a small gully. The rolling barrage which we had followed up the hill had carried on but was now coming back in our direction...we just kept as low as possible, and it passed through us.'

Between 80 and 82 rounds were being fired at the patrol by 7 (Sphinx) Battery, 29 Commando Regiment, Royal Artillery. The Forward Observation Officer, directing the artillery fire was Captain Willy McCracken. It had a devastating effect. By now, 9 of the 14-man patrol were injured. The situation was pretty desperate.

Over the next 40 minutes, three members of the Patrol, including one injured soldier, managed to crawl up over Fisherman's Valley as the barrage continued, and came into the 7 (Sphinx) Battery position by Findlay Rocks, where they were evacuated by 'Bandwagon 202', a tracked articulated arctic vehicle. But for the remainder, still in Fisherman's Valley, the artillery and small arms fire continued.

It was around 12.17 that Major Osborne, Officer Commanding C Company suspected that the A Company patrol was lost, possibly 1000metres from its reported position, and that what had been occurring was a 'Blue on Blue' engagement. Firing which had lasted for nearly 35 minutes finally stopped. The Commanding Officer appreciating the need for urgent medical support, arranged for a helicopter to evacuate them. John Hare and his colleagues, still in the valley, were still anticipating the worst....

> 'There was then silence and I remember Corporal Duggan saying, 'They will probably follow up and finish us off now so John, you cover that direction, Ginge this way and I will cover here.' Just then Private Etches, (also wounded) crawled into our position. We tended aid to him, and (we) then heard the sound of helicopters'

The agony didn't end there as the first Sea King helicopter approached too fast, attempted a fan stop and crash landed, ploughing its tail rotor into a downward slope of a rise in the ground. The second helicopter picked up 8 casualties and took them onto HMS Intrepid, instead of Ajax Bay, where the field hospital was stood by to receive them. One of John Hare's abiding memories of the flight was of blood swilling about on the helicopter deck as the casualties lay in agony, cold, wet, hungry and traumatized.

The rest of 2 Troop only learnt of what had happened when Ginge Hall staggered back into our line of trenches later that afternoon. Apart from being informed that John Hare had been shot and was being evacuated, the Troop had little understanding of the terrible chaos that

CHAPTER 10

had unfolded over the previous hours. Ginge Hall was understandably very shaken up by what he had endured. It was a reminder, if one was needed, of the fog of war, and of how even a professional battalion like 3 Para could get things badly wrong.

Remarkably, and thanks to a very large extent to the wonderful work of Commander Rick Jolly and his surgical team at Ajax Bay, all the Blue-on-Blue casualties survived. What of John Hare's recovery?

> *'I woke up in Ajax Bay and felt terrible, and when I pulled the blanket down to see what the strange feeling was on my stomach, I was shocked to see some of my intestines in a plastic bag.'* He was on a stretcher on trestles right next to the operating theatre. *'You could see right over to the operating area and the surgeons in the rubber aprons, some with helmets on. The place was bombed whilst I was there.'*

He was eventually moved onto HMS Uganda which sailed to Montevideo, where casualties were transferred to RAF VC 10 for the flight home, via Ascension Island. He made a full recovery, and subsequently served with distinction until retiring in 2000 to become a Director of BACTEC, the commercial mine clearance company. In recent years, he has been clearing minefields left behind by the Argentinians during the 1982 conflict. John was awarded the MBE in the New Year's Honours List 2022 for his remarkable contribution to the Falkland Islands over many years.

Whilst there have been calls to apportion blame for the 23rd of May 'Blue on Blue' incident, it is worth reflecting on John Hare's comments some years later before making any judgements.

'I don't blame anyone for what happened. It's not the first time and for sure it hasn't been the last time as we all know. It's unfortunate but we can thank the stars we made it back. I am grateful every day to the helicopter pilots, medics, surgeons, doctors and nurses who saved us.'

Map showing the landings on the 21st of May and the enemy positions on Fanning Head.

CHAPTER 10

A 105mm Light Gun from 7 (Sphinx) Battery. Around 82 rounds were fired at the A Company patrol in the 23rd of May blue-on-blue incident.

Casualties from the blue-on-blue incident were initially flown onto HMS Intrepid, before being transferred to the field surgical facility at Ajax Bay.

Surgeon Commander Rick Jolly outside the surgical facility at Ajax Bay. Every casualty who made it to his surgery survived.

Chapter 11

THE MARCH EAST

By the 29th of May, the Battalion was under orders for a rapid march East. Our objective was Estancia, a settlement 50 miles away, and only 15 miles from Port Stanley. It would be from Estancia, that preparations and planning for the Battle for Mount Longdon would take place. For 2 Troop, it was also time to select a team of around 40 for the march. The reduced size troop consisted of 3 field sections and a Troop Headquarters team, with Jock Ferry, Scott Wilson and Mick Humphries leading each of the field sections. Mick had replaced Corporal Kev Cowling, who had struggled to impose his authority on the Section. The remainder of the Troop would remain at Port San Carlos to support the more substantial engineer forces coming in behind.

The reduced and streamlined group from 2 Troop was a tough and uncompromising team, fit and focused. News that we were to move East with 3 Para galvanised everyone. Morale was high, even though we were moving into unknown territory with a battalion we barely knew. We had already worked out for ourselves that the quickest way back home was to capture the capital, Port Stanley, take the Argentinian surrender and then get back on a ship. The sooner that was going to happen, the better.

Our initial journey East was by Rigid Raider for some 4 miles up the meandering San Carlos River. From there, we were on our feet, moving with Patrols Company for most of the way, across moorland in biting cold and wet weather. At times advancing ahead of the rest of the battalion, it was a weird feeling, moving forward in daylight and darkness without a clear understanding of enemy locations. The prospect of coming under enemy fire was ever present. The advance was also tough going. We were carrying full kit with bergans, weapons, ammunition, mine clearance equipment, explosive charges, hand tools, rations and water. No-one had less than 80 lbs on their backs. The temperature hovered around 0-3 degrees C, with a constant, cutting wind and rain which turned to sleet. A brief stop in open countryside with no cover during the first night provided little relief! From what I can remember, we just huddled together in the rain and the wind until daybreak.

The second night offered the prospect of some shelter at Teal Inlet. Whilst we marched East to Teal Inlet, our friends from 2 Para were heading South to Goose Green.

GOOSE GREEN

The battle for Goose Green took place on the 28th and 29th of May. 2 Para, supported by Recce Troop, 59 Independent Commando Squadron, fought a six phase, night/day silent-noisy battalion attack

CHAPTER 11

against formidable forces well dug-in around Darwin and Goose Green. The Battalion benefitted from modest artillery support from only three 105mm guns and Naval Gunfire Support from HMS Arrow that was subject to mechanical issues and was withdrawn at a critical stage of the battle. Their plans were compromised on the night of the 27th of May by a BBC World Service news bulletin announcement that 2 Para were now within 5 miles of Darwin. So, with enemy forces forewarned and reinforced, the Battalion fought valiantly to secure the settlement and release the local inhabitants, who had been kept hostage in the schoolhouse throughout the battle. The British casualty list was high, with 17 dead, including Lieutenant Colonel H Jones, the Commanding Officer, and 35 wounded. With 450 men, they had prevailed over a force four times their own strength.

It was as we approached Teal Inlet that the disturbing news was picked up on the Brigade radio network. Reports of the Goose Green casualties left the whole Battalion Group in sombre mood. For me personally, news that my close friend, Jim Barry, had died along with another friend from Kenya, Chris Dent, Lieutenant Colonel H Jones, and his adjutant, Captain David Wood was keenly felt. Jim Barry was killed at Goose Green during a combined assault by both C and D Companies to secure the schoolhouse. It was whilst responding to an enemy white flag and taking the surrender of a group of Argentinians that Jim was gunned down. News of the death of Corporal Mick Melia, formally a section commander in 2 Troop, but recently posted to 59 Squadron's Recce Troop, also weighed heavily. Mick was hugely respected in 9 Squadron and badly missed by the Troop. It didn't pass us by that Mick was supporting 2 Para, the Battalion that 2 Troop should have been supporting, had there not been late changes to the plan. Recce Troop, under the command of Lieutenant Clive Livingstone, excelled in the adversity of the Goose Green battle. I wondered if 2 Troop was heading for a similar engagement on our slog to Stanley, and if so, how we would perform. In the rain and the darkness on the night of the 30th of May, gloom descended on us all.

The next day, we set off East again, supporting Patrols Company. As the Battalion approached Estancia, a classic example of the misuse of combat engineers unfolded. One of the fields approaching Estancia House had clearly been mined by the enemy. Dead cows and sheep littered the field, which was on the line of approach for the Battalion. Orders arrived with Patrols Company that the sappers were to 'clear a route through the field'. Jock Ferry, a meticulous and professional field engineer, pointed out that this procedure, if carried out properly, would take 6 to 8 hours. 'You have one hour, get on with it!' was the reply. Realising that this was not the time to debate the issue, he assembled a group of engineers and paratroopers and simply marched forward with them, line abreast, creating a cleared route about 8 metres wide. It was a very high-risk solution to the problem.

CHAPTER 11

It was also a brave and thankless task. By a stroke of luck, they took no casualties.

REINFORCEMENTS ARRIVE

Fifth Infantry Brigade set sail on the Queen Elizabeth the 2nd, on the 12th of May. On board was 2nd Battalion, the Scots Guards, 1st Battalion, the Welsh Guards, 1st/7th Duke of Edinburgh's Own Gurkha Rifles, 97 Field Battery, Royal Artillery, 656 Squadron, Army Air Corps, 16 Field Ambulance and 9 Parachute Squadron Royal Engineers. After cross-decking onto MV Norland and SS Canberra at South Georgia, the Brigade landed at San Carlos on the 1st and 2nd of June.

The plan was to establish a second, Southern axis in order to develop a divisional operation to secure the mountains around Stanley. First, the Brigade was to establish itself at Goose Green, some 15 miles South of the San Carlos landing sites. The advance to Goose Green on foot proved challenging for the Welsh Guards, who returned back over Sussex Mountain on the 3rd of June after a 10-hour slog in the rain. This confirmed the view that 5 Infantry Brigade was unable to move on foot with all its necessary equipment to Fitzroy and Bluff Cove. With the vast majority of the available helicopter assets already committed to providing logistic support for 3 Commando Brigade, strung out along the Northern axis, the only viable alternative was to move 5 Brigade's infantry by sea.

Following their success at Goose Green, 2 Para was placed under the new brigade. Elements of A and B Companies advanced to Fitzroy by helicopter in a daring raid having ascertained by telephone call to the settlement that the enemy had left the area.

RFA SIR GALAHAD

On the night of the 5th/6th June, the Scots Guards were moved forward to Fitzroy through heavy seas. The following night, the 6th/7th of June, 2 companies of the Welsh Guards underwent the same sea journey to Fitzroy, first by HMS Fearless and then by LCU, again in appalling weather. But 300 Guardsmen, together with elements of 16 Field Ambulance and 4 Troop, 9 Parachute Squadron, could not be transferred ashore by first light and returned with the assault ship back to the protection of San Carlos Water.

At 7am on the 8th of June, LSL Sir Galahad, with the remaining elements of the Welsh Guards, along with 16 Field Ambulance and 4 Troop, dropped anchor at Fitzroy. Whilst disembarking, the LSL was attacked by 4 Argentinian aircraft,

CHAPTER 11

2 Mirages and 2 Skyhawks. Her sister ship, Sir Tristram was also at anchor in the bay and also found herself under attack. Fifty one men lost their lives in the attack including Corporal McIlvenny and Sapper Tarbard from 9 Squadron. A further eight members 4 Troop were injured in the attack. The same day, the LCU 'Foxtrot 4' was bombed and sunk as she transited along the Southern coast of East Falkland, with the loss of 6 lives, and HMS Plymouth was badly damaged in a further air attack in Falkland Sound.

Chapter 12

ESTANCIA

News of the Fitzroy attacks and their tragic consequences trickled in. In the Troop, we were unaware that fellow Royal Engineers from 9 Parachute Squadron were involved. Indeed, we had no idea where our parent Squadron was. The loss of life was a further reminder that, although our battalion had come through the first two weeks of the conflict largely unscathed, that was unlikely to continue. I managed to secure a Gazelle helicopter lift to Fitzroy a couple of days after the attack to catch up with 9 Squadron, exchange information on the enemy and particularly to share what we knew about the Argentinian minefields. RFAs Sir Galahad and Sir Tristram were still at anchor in the inlet, smouldering away. I was met with mixed emotions on being re-united with Squadron second-in-command Freddie Kemp and fellow troop commanders Richard Willett and Jon Mullin. Clearly, the events of the 8th of June were foremost in their minds. The Squadron had been at the heart of the casualty evacuation activity after the air raid and had discovered the fate of 4 Troop only when they began transferring their casualties to the impromptu dressing station at Fitzroy settlement. Why had it taken so long to get units off the Galahad? Why were LSLs allowed to drop anchor in broad daylight, unprotected by any anti-aircraft cover? As I learnt, 4 Troop, the newly attached Troop from 20 Field Squadron had experienced the full horrors of the bombing raid on Galahad. And the Squadron Headquarters, established on land right next to the inlet, had been early on the scene and instrumental in organising the response. I sensed the shock, the anger and the frustration, but also a palpable keenness to get involved in the fight ahead. In an odd way, I was glad to re-board the helicopter and return to the relative order of life at Estancia.

Life at Estancia House was surreal. It was like the waiting room at a dental practice. Everyone knew that something very painful was going to happen shortly, but no-one wanted to talk about it. These were critical days of preparation, of gathering intelligence, of briefings and orders and of rehearsals. The Troop dug in again but also made use of some tarpaulin provided by the wonderful Tony Heathman, the local farmer, to construct shelters from the relentless wind and rain.

Nightly battalion patrols East to the Murrell River and the base of Mount Longdon were supported by elements of the Troop. Taff Sweeney was involved in several patrols as was Jock Ferry, Scott Wilson, Jonah Jones and Mick Humphries. Taff remembers three such patrols, characterised by a tough march into the Longdon area, a delicate approach march close to enemy positions, and on the third such patrol, wading across the freezing-cold Murrell River and finding the edge of one of three poorly

CHAPTER 12

marked minefields below the mountain. 'They were marked simply with stone piles,' he remembered four decades later, being so close that... 'We could hear and see the enemy infantry'. Others recalled one patrol when the group was fired at from the adjacent mountain, Two Sisters, and then from Mount Longdon itself. Extraction from a difficult situation was achieved by calling in artillery fire support, whilst scrambling into dead ground.

It is almost impossible to explain to those who have not done it, what it was like to have the responsibility of locating enemy minefields. As engineers taking part in a fighting patrol, sappers were expected to be able to undertake this task on top of all the skills required of a top-class infantryman. It was the infantry's job to get us close to the enemy's defensive position undetected, and our job to locate the minefield. Yet the chances of success were miniscule, despite our training. Argentine anti-personnel mines were made from plastic and were undetectable using traditional mine clearing equipment, which only detected metal objects. Instead, the Troop had to resort to the old and unsophisticated method, using minefield 'prodders'. These were little more than a spike with a handle. If a prodder wasn't available, we used our bayonets. Whilst the Geneva Convention required combatants to place these mines within a marked and fenced minefield, the Argentinians had not followed this Convention. As Taff Sweeney recalled, if the Troop was lucky, they would come across stone piles marking the extremities of the minefield. More often than not the minefields were completely unmarked. Add to this mix the moorland terrain in which mines had been buried, and the fact that patrols were carried out at night, in cold, inclement weather and it's perhaps easy to begin to appreciate how the odds were often stacked against us.

The Argentinians had placed their protective minefields within a few hundred metres of their own trenches, and unbeknown to us, the Argentine infantry platoons were equipped with the latest technology in thermal imaging night sights. So, there was a very real prospect of sappers being seen by the enemy whilst ferreting around close to their defensive positions. This was the case on one such patrol, when Lance Corporal Jonah Jones managed to retrieve an anti-tank mine and haul it back to Estancia for examination. It was a remarkable achievement, not least because anti-tank mines were laid in such a pattern that each was surrounded by a number of largely undetectable anti-personnel mines. The inadvertent pressure of an elbow on one such mine would have been terminal for Jonah and would have compromised his fighting patrol. To find this anti-tank mine, buried in the peat, and to extract it, in full view of the enemy, took real courage. It was a pre-meditated act, not a spur of the moment, spontaneous response to events as they unfolded. The consequences of just the slightest wrong move, or simply a piece of bad luck, were fully understood by Jonah. Unsurprisingly, on the night he rescued the anti-tank mine, his patrol was indeed seen and engaged by the enemy as it extracted itself back to safety.

CHAPTER 12

For Mick Humphries, the 10th of June was a significant day, his wedding anniversary. To celebrate whilst on sentry duty at Estancia, he crouched down in the bottom of his wet trench and smoked his last cigar, saved for the occasion. Forty years later, he recalls writing a letter to his wife Chris that evening. In it he made a request that, were he not to return home, she would pledge to ensure that his son never became a 'craphat'! (non-airborne soldier).

The relentless patrols programme took its toll, and after a solid week of them, all those involved were feeling the pressure. Tired, wet, and stressed, all of us were aware that this was but the prelude to the battle ahead.

The author – 'Troopie', during the march to Estancia.

BELONGING TO 2 TROOP

Steve Wildman, Scott Wilson and the author check out their feet.

A break from the march to Estancia.
Steve Lobban, Steve Wildman, Taff Preston and Scott Wilson.

CHAPTER 12

Corporal Scott Wilson.

11th of June. Final preparations for the Battle for Mount Longdon. The white tape is being prepared to provide markers for the Battalion start line and for any identified enemy minefields.

11th of June. Final preparations for the Battle for Mount Longdon.

CHAPTER 12

RFA Sir Galahad, following the air attack on the 8th of June 1982.

THE DIVISIONAL ATTACKS ONTO THE MOUNTAINS AROUND PORT STANLEY

In early June, with British Forces now occupying Mount Kent, Mount Challenger and Mount Estancia, the challenge of overcoming the enemy surrounding Stanley looked daunting. Thirty-three company groups had been identified in the hills West of the capital, in a garrison force of around 8,400 men, dug in with plentiful ammunition and supported by heavy artillery. On the 8th of June, a few hours before the Galahad was attacked, Major General Moore agreed his plan for the breakthrough to Stanley. It would be a two-brigade operation with 3 Commando Brigade launched first to secure Mount Longdon

(3 Para's objective), Two Sisters (45 Commando's objective) and Mount Harriet (42 Commando's objective). The following night, the three infantry battalions of 5 Infantry Brigade would comprise phase 2. The Scots Guards, the Welsh Guards and the Gurkhas would pass through 3 Commando Brigade to attack Mount Tumbledown, Mount William and subsequently Sapper Hill. The first wave of the operation commenced on the night of the 11th/12th of June and by mid-day on the 12th of June, all objectives had been secured. The 5 Infantry Brigade's assaults were delayed 24 hours whilst sufficient artillery and ammunition was brought forward by helicopter. But on the night of the 13th/14th of June, their assault was launched, with the addition of an attack onto Wireless Ridge in the North by 2 Para.

Chapter 13

MOUNT LONGDON

The 11th of June arrived and the advance to the Murrell River and onto Mount Longdon was in everyone's minds. The Battalion Orders Group that morning was followed by more detailed company and platoon briefings. Final preparations for the Troop included distributing key items of engineer equipment between each section and rehearsing how we might tackle previously unidentified minefields. Plastic explosives, detonators, minefield clearance kit, additional ammunition, grenades, rations, water and first aid kit all had to be fitted into bergans and webbing. Anything not vital for the battle ahead was ditched. What to carry and what to leave behind was keenly debated.

As we understood it, the plan was to conduct a silent night attack with H-Hour timed for 8.01pm. The Battalion would attack from the North West with B Company under command of Major Mike Argue given the objective of the immediate summit, nicknamed 'Fly Half', with the aim of then fighting along the ridgeline to the second summit, known as 'Full Back'. A Company (Major David Collett) would advance to the left of B Company on the Northern side of the mountain and occupy a prominent spur of high ground, nicknamed 'Wing Forward'. C Company was to be in reserve.

Support Company had considerable firepower at its disposal to support the rifle companies, including 5 Milan firing posts, 5 SF Machine guns, and our own troop 0.30 inch Browning machine gun. Mortar Platoon equipped with six 81mm 'tubes' would be on call. In addition, the Battalion had a battery of light guns from 29 Commando Regiment and Naval Gunfire Support in the form of the frigate HMS Avenger's 4.5-inch gun. The NGFO was Captain Willy McCracken who was to move initially with B Company.

These were tense times, and each of us dealt with our demons in different ways. It was obvious to all after the casualty count at Goose Green that some would not survive the night and that others would receive life changing injuries. Many were in reflective mood. It helped that the business of preparing for the advance filled much of the final hours. A last hot meal, a bit of banter, and then an uncomfortable silence filled the air. There was nothing more to talk about.

At 5pm local time, as dusk descended, the Battalion began its 7 km march to the foot of Mount Longdon. Packs on, weapons ready, cam cream on, final checks, whispered instructions, lining up, counting off. The Troop had been closely involved in identifying the start lines for each company's attack in the preceding 11 days of reconnaissance with D (Patrols) Company. Now, each section was attached to one of the three rifle companies, whilst Troop Headquarters advanced with Support

CHAPTER 13

Company, escorting 4 Volvo BV 202Es, six tractors and nine civilian land rovers. These vehicles were carrying mortar, Milan and GPMG ammunition, vital for the forthcoming battle. Also, in the convoy was the secondary Regimental Aid Post, including a doctor and two medics. It was a cold, wet night and the approach march was a slow, stop-start snake of men carrying heavy weapons and ammunition, endured for the most part in silence. For the Troop, carrying explosives and demining equipment and a selection of engineer hand tools, we were each carrying bergans weighing in at 80lbs plus. Keeping pace with our infantry counterparts was tough.

A key role allocated to the Troop was to help each company get across the Murrell River – its bridge having already been badly damaged. Although not much more than a stream in spate, it was our job to ensure that the infantry got to the start line in as good a condition as possible. Initially, demolition ladders were to be used, subsequently to be replaced by a more substantial structure. But how to hold the ladders in place whilst 400 soldiers stepped across? Jock Ferry had the answer. Strip off, get into the stream up to your waist and hold the ladders firm from underneath. This he did for minutes on end until he had lost all feeling in his legs. Although numbers of men crossed using this improvised bridge, the bottleneck created forced B Company to take a more direct route to their start line.

In truth, the Troop was hardly used at all in our engineer role throughout that night and the following day. Perhaps that's no surprise. The battle that followed was a close quarter fight which would have been familiar to any infantryman who had fought in the two World Wars. For the field sections of 2 Troop, all they could do is fight with their affiliated companies, provide whatever support they could and ride their luck.

Facing 3 Para on Mount Longdon was B Company of the Argentinian 7th Infantry Regiment (RI7), reinforced with a Special Forces detachment. They were as young as the 3 Para toms and had been recruited from Buenos Aires. They had arrived on East Falkland on the 13th of April and had moved up onto Mount Longdon the next day. They were well equipped with FN rifles, an automatic version of the SLR that we carried, and they had received one year's training. In support, they had a heavy machine gun company with excellent large calibre 12.7mm machine guns, anti-tank crews with both recoilless rifles and guided missiles, and 81mm and 120mm mortars. Occupying the high ground and well dug in, they represented a formidable obstacle.

The defenders of Mount Longdon had spent 6 weeks preparing their defensive positions before our arrival at the Battalion start line. They had laid mines around the hill, largely unmarked, but had not thought through how to cover these obstacles with supporting fire. Although many of their trenches were well constructed and difficult to identify, they had not used barbed wire, sandbags, and other field defences to good effect. Crucially, there had also been little attempt to protect their positions by aggressive patrolling ahead of the battle.

Sapper Sam Robson's experience was typical of many in the Troop that night. Sam was supporting B

CHAPTER 13

Company, commanded by Major Mike Argue. Sam had been on several of the night patrols on the preceding nights and so had the task of guiding the Company around Argentinian close protection minefields and into position on their start line, along with Corporal Phillips and Lance Corporal Wright of Patrols Company. Sam also had the job of tackling any obstacles or booby traps they might encounter. The Company was slightly late into position because of problems on the approach march. It was a cold, clear night, close to full moon, with frost beginning to form on the tussocks of grass they lay in. Although he had no doubt about what lay ahead, Sam was nevertheless still galvanised when he received the order to 'fix bayonets!' His immediate thought was 'Fuck me, this is it.' Indeed, it was.

Sam found himself with 6 Platoon, commanded by Lieutenant Jon Shaw. Their initial progress up the Western slope of Mount Longdon was remarkable. A silent approach through what were later established as Argentine positions. The silence was shattered when Corporal Milne stood on a mine. Once the alarm had been raised amongst the enemy locations, the platoon ran up the remaining slope, by-passing enemy bunkers, to secure their objective, known as 'Fly Half'. A fierce fire fight ensued, with a number of the Platoon killed or injured in the following hour. Sam recalls at one stage being instructed to look after Private Dodsworth, one of the Company medics, who had been shot next to him. Private Steve Richards had already attempted to stem his bleeding using a shell dressing, which had quickly filled to capacity. Sam did his best to comfort him and keep him warm as the firefight ensued. 6 Platoon's desperate, close quarter battle continued throughout the night. Hemmed in amongst the rocks and being fired upon at close range, they showed immense courage to edge forward, win the fire fight and secure the position.

Corporal Jock Ferry's section supported A Company that night. He recalls them coming under fire for the first time, with his section about 60 meters behind Company Headquarters. Initially taking cover in the heather, they were then encouraged to keep moving. Once on their feet again, they came across a man lying face down. Assuming that he just needed a little encouragement, Jock tapped him on the feet and said, 'Come on, get moving!' It then became apparent that he had been fatally wounded with a bullet to the head. Although the Orders Group had earlier emphasised the need to leave casualties and keep the momentum of the assault, Jock, along with Sapper Pete Poulson, dragged the injured man back to his Company Sergeant Major, some distance behind Company Headquarters and then ran forward to catch up with the advance. (The injured man was Corporal Stevie Hope. He succumbed to his injuries and is buried in Aldershot Military Cemetery). The remainder of Jock's night was spent edging forward, crawling, laying low, crawling again, directly behind Company Headquarters, as the battle continued. He was frustrated because his men were under-utilised for much of the night.

During the night, Troop Headquarters found itself escorting the Regimental Aid Post, consisting of two BV

CHAPTER 13

202s, through the minefield and up to the Western edge of the mountain. In full view of the enemy on Two Sisters, we were unsurprisingly engaged by artillery fire along the Murrell River. We then eased through the minefield and managed to bring the Regimental Aid Post into position by a rough outcrop of rocks a few hundred metres from the summit before daylight.

One engineer task that Jock Ferry and Mick Humphries had to deal with that night was an Argentinian booby-trapped bunker. Jock used his initiative and 100 metres of parachute cord to hook up the devise and yank it out of the bunker. Having rendered it safe and marked it with mine tape, he later discovered that it was a thermal battery pack for a Surface-to-Air (SAM) 7 missile, set up to look like a booby trap!

By first light, Sapper Mark (Tommy) Trindall found himself helping casualties around a feature known as the First Bowl. He was alongside Corporal Scott Wilson and Sapper Steve Tickle. They were briefly reflecting on their experiences of the night battle when a high-pitched noise was followed by an enormous explosion about 15 metres away, on the eastern face of the bowl. Tommy remembers rolling into a ball, being covered in dirt and rocks and then uncurling, head spinning as a result of the noise. Miraculously, Tommy was unscathed, but Scott, just a metre away, had caught the blast, and was fatally wounded. Together with Steve, Tommy tried mouth to mouth resuscitation. They were soon to receive blunt advice from a nearby medic. Scott was dead, he told them, and they needed to move on and help carry the rest of the wounded to the Regimental Aid Post. What exactly had caused the explosion wasn't clear. Some believe it was a 120mm mortar round, others that it may have been a HEAT (High Explosive Anti-Tank) round from a 105mm recoilless rifle located on the Western edge of Wireless Ridge.

Scott was a remarkable soldier. Had he lived, he would have almost certainly advanced to Warrant Officer (Class 1) and been commissioned. He was an enormously positive force within the Troop, kind and generous with the younger sappers, humorous, thoughtful and deeply loyal. He was literally the heart and soul of the Troop and his loss was felt hugely by us all. By a sad twist of fate, Scott's brother-in-law, Ginge McCarthy, a Corporal in the Milan Platoon of 3 Para, had died 90 minutes earlier, on the same hill. Scott and Jock Ferry had found his body and marked where he fell with his rifle and helmet, only for Scott to be killed shortly afterwards giving aid to casualties.

Dawn on the 12th of June was a welcome relief, but it didn't stop the sporadic artillery and mortar fire dropping down on the Troop's newly secured positions. Indeed, with 'Full Back' now secure, the Argentinian artillery on the outskirts of Port Stanley targeted the whole mountain, with fire being directed from Mount Tumbledown, adjacent to us and still in enemy hands. Mount Longdon was an unpleasant place to hunker down and try and find shelter from the continuing bombardment. In amongst the Troop were Argentinian prisoners, also desperate for cover from their own artillery. Some were in a very poor state; bewildered, cold, hungry and scared. Humanity

CHAPTER 13

demanded that they be invited into the rock sangers we now occupied. There they lay, huddled alongside toms and sappers. We shared our 'brews' with those who had been our enemies a few hours before. Another long and murderous night followed, interrupted by shellfire and cries of 'medic', as brave souls dived out of their shelters to lift and drag casualties down the hill.

One such individual was Sapper Butch Glover. Butch was a strong character in a troop full of strong characters. Tough, fit, athletic, quick witted and entertaining, he was a man with obvious potential. On the morning of the 12th of June, he was assisting with casualty recovery and the removal of the dead. As a stretcher bearer, he carried Private Grant Grinham, in considerable pain, to the RAP, which by then was overflowing with wounded. Then he turned around and went back up the hill with body bags to zip up the battalion dead and stretcher them down. At this point, he learnt that his mentor and boss for the past two years, Scott Wilson, had just been killed. The news was very hard to take for Butch.

Soon after Scott's death, I was summoned to see the Commanding Officer at his Tactical Headquarters further up the mountain. It was only 100 metres away and consisted of Lieutenant Colonel Pike, his RSM, his signallers and a couple of close protection guys. He kindly took the time to pass on his condolences. 'I am sorry for the loss of Corporal Wilson', he said. 'He was a fine soldier'. I could do little more than agree and to thank him. On reflection, this was impressive stuff from a great commanding officer. By the morning of the 12th of June, he had lost 19 soldiers with a further 45 injured. But he took time to consider his attached sappers.

Our accommodation amongst the rocks was in the form of sangers built of stones. Taff Sweeney and I shared one tight in against an outcrop, which slanted at an angle, providing protection of some sort against the Argentinian artillery. I returned to Mount Longdon 10 years later, whilst commanding my Regiment. I was visiting one of my Squadrons on a 6-month deployment to the Falkland Islands and had joined a group of soldiers conducting a battlefield tour. Whilst wandering around listening to the presentations, I located my own sanger from 1982. I couldn't resist the urge to scramble into it. There in the bottom of it, I found a green bungee I had left there a decade previously. I had bought it in Halfords the year before the conflict and used it to suspend my groundsheet and convert it into a makeshift tent or 'basher'. I looked at it and wryly reflected on whether Halfords knew what a significant contribution they had made to our victory in the Falklands!

There were some bizarre events that stick in the memory for those on that hill over those few days. For me personally, it was the arrival of the mail later that afternoon. A scout helicopter had crept forward, using the folds in the ground for cover, and landed on the Western end of the mountain under artillery fire in order to get a couple of the critically injured casualties away. As it landed, rotors turning, out were thrown two mail bags. It was 2 Troop's mail! I hadn't seen any mail for weeks, so I was astonished and bemused in equal measure to discover that included in one of the bags were some 15 or

CHAPTER 13

so 'blueys', (airmail letters) from my fiancée, my mother, father, sister and other relatives dating back to late April. With occasional artillery rounds incoming, I quietly read each one over a brew.

Sporadic artillery fire rained on us throughout a cold day on the 13th of June. It had been a bitter night and a light dusting of snow covered the mountain. The detritus of war was still everywhere. Abandoned weapons, clothing, sleeping bags, rations, bodies, empty cases and munitions boxes littered the position. The Troop was low on water by then, and we scuttled around to find what was available in amongst the peaty bogs. I remember my first night in Port Stanley after the surrender being violently ill, projectile vomiting, probably as a consequence of the conditions of our time on Longdon.

The night of the 13th of June was a significant improvement on the previous two nights. The enemy's artillery fire had largely moved away, focusing on defending their positions on Wireless Ridge and the impending attack onto Mount Tumbledown to our South. 2 Para's assault onto Wireless ridge was underway. It was supported by tremendous artillery, naval gunfire and direct fire support from the Scorpions of the Blues and Royals. It was impressive stuff, and it was soon obvious what the outcome was likely to be. As it concluded, and dawn arrived. the Troop was, at last, tasked with re-enforcing C Company on a new objective. Hew Pike explained that his rifle companies had taken a battering over the previous 48 hours, and that we were to move into the infantry role and act as a platoon. C Company was commanded by Major Martin Osborne and its three platoons were 7, 8 and 9 Platoon. As I understood it, the Company's objective was to have been Moody Brook Barracks on the edge of Port Stanley. This was to be a daylight attack across open countryside. It had the potential to be tricky. I am not sure we had time to meet up with the Company before I gave the Troop a Warning Order about the task ahead of us. Our briefing session that morning was remarkable. Realisation that we were to be in the front line of the next battalion attack galvanised everyone into action. It seemed to me that the news was met with resolve and determination, despite the experiences of the preceding 72 hours. We would be fighting together as a troop, not farmed out to others as combat engineer sections. Allocating us this important task was empowering. In a funny way it was an invitation to join our new family. Belonging to 3 Para had become immeasurably important to us all.

By happy co-incidence, news of a potential ceasefire started to filter across the mountain shortly afterwards. We didn't get the chance to meet up with C Company as before long, orders were revised, and the Troop was tasked with a rapid march into Stanley itself. In single file, we left our positions amongst the rocks of Mount Longdon and marched East, edging through the last of the minefields, with spirits high. Losing ground quickly, we passed Wireless Ridge, which 2 Para had just captured, to our left and dropped down to Moody Brook Barracks. A few hours previously, it had been the focus of our next offensive. And then we eased along the road littered with the detritus of war and into Port Stanley.

CHAPTER 13

Map of 3 Para's route from Port San Carlos to Port Stanley, a distance of 62 miles taken on foot.

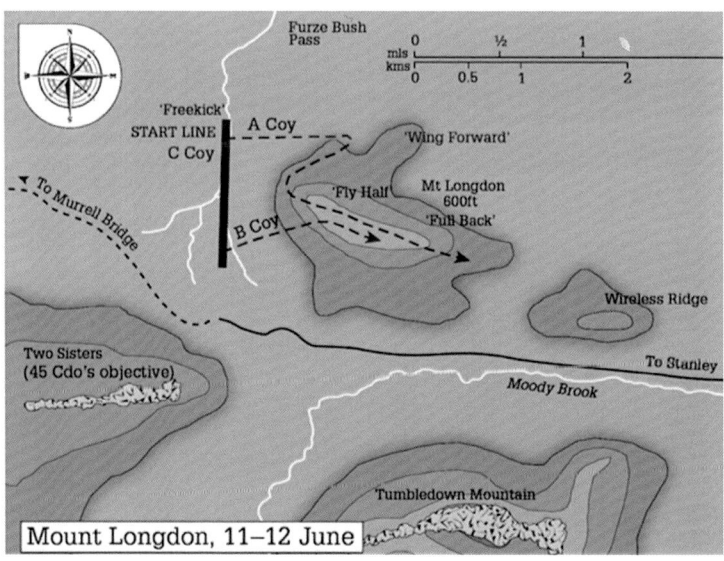

Map of Mount Longdon, 11-12 June 1982.

First aid being administered to Argentine casualties on Mount Longdon, the 12th of June 1982.

Argentine prisoners of war under guard. The 12th of June 1982. The Troop HQ sanger was up the hill, top right.

CHAPTER 13

Prisoners of war being searched for weapons.

*Daylight on the 12th of June. Lance Corporal
Mick Humphries manages a grim smile.*

BELONGING TO 2 TROOP

Mount Longdon – The 12th of June 1982. Casualties being assembled at the Regimental Aid Post for helicopter evacuation.

Mount Longdon. The 12th of June 1982. Mick Leather with a captured Argentinian 50mm machine gun.

CHAPTER 13

The morning of the 14th of June 1982. Five members of the Troop shortly before the Argentine surrender. From left to right – Smudge Smith, Ginge Moore, Dill Rodgers, Nick Preston and Sam Robson.

2 Troop hear news of the Argentine surrender. The 14th of June 1982.

The Troop's first glimpse of Port Stanley from the summit of Mount Longdon.

The memorial plaque to Corporal Scott Wilson, near the spot where he was killed on Mount Longdon.

CHAPTER 13

Past and present members of 9 Parachute Squadron pay their respects to Scott Wilson on Mount Longdon. Present in the photograph are Freddie Kemp, (Squadron 2ic in in 1982), and John Hare and Derek Broadbent from 2 Troop (1982).

Chapter 14

PORT STANLEY

THE SURRENDER

The Argentine Commander, General Menendes formally surrendered to Lieutenant Colonel Rose, 22 SAS at Government House Port Stanley on the afternoon of the 14th of June 1982. General Jeremy Moore, Commanding the British troops and his Argentine counterpart put their signatures to the surrender document at 9pm (local). Back in London, at 10.15pm, Mrs Thatcher rose from her seat in the House of Commons and, much to the relief and joy of members, made the following statement, 'Our forces have reached the outskirts of Port Stanley. Large numbers of Argentine soldiers threw down their weapons. They are reported to be flying white flags over Port Stanley.'

Although Stanley was a welcome sight, it was also a macabre experience. A few Argentinian bodies lined the route into the town from the East, and distraught Argentinian prisoners-of-war gathered in groups.

Their weapons were being dumped into piles on the main street, whilst lines of British troops were pouring in off the nearby mountainsides. The Troop's first concern was to find a place to use as a base. We eased into the small wooden tabernacle chapel and settled in. Jock Ferry improvised a bed out of a stack of bibles, complete with raised pillow. God helps those who help themselves! The chapel had running water and was dry. At last, the guys were out of the relentless wind and rain. Fabulous!

By the next morning, 3 Para's interest in 2 Troop reduced to pretty much zero. We were on our own again, to meet up with 59 Squadron, and in due course, 9 Squadron, who had landed as part of 5 Infantry Brigade. Never short of initiative, the Troop worked out quickly that to be effective in this post conflict period, we needed transport. With only a little encouragement from me, teams went out and searched for any motor transport they could apprehend. Within 3 hours, a convoy of 35 vehicles had been assembled outside the chapel. At its head was Argentine General Menendez' staff car, a rather smart Mercedes. Mick Humphries had come across it, with its engine ticking over, outside Government House, the Governor General's residence on the West side of the town. The Argentinian General was busy inside surrendering to General Jeremy Moore, his British counterpart. Menendez' driver, still armed with a pistol, sat waiting for his leader to come out when Mick encouraged him (by pointing his rifle through the window) to get out and join his mates in the prisoner queue! Mick was very proud later that afternoon to present 'Troopie' with his new wheels.

CHAPTER 14

In Port Stanley, the clear up started and our combat engineering skills were badly needed. Immediately after the ceasefire, and still under command of 59 Independent Commando Squadron, we were first tasked to clear the landmines on Yorke Bay, North-West of Port Stanley. Yorke Bay is a sandy cove and was ideal for bringing much needed stores ashore after the conflict. Sergeant Taff Sweeney had been briefed by the Intelligence Section of 59 Squadron, and had been given the Argentine Engineers Minefield Records, showing the pattern, depth, type, and number of mines laid in each row across the Bay. We organised the Troop into small clearance sections, each with specific tasks, to locate, uncover, count and eventually neutralise each landmine. They were then lifted and carried to a marked safe area, for subsequent disposal. Eventually the beach was declared safe for use. Colleagues in 59 Squadron were doing the same tasks elsewhere, resulting unfortunately in two separate incidents where unidentified mines exploded resulting in two sappers losing limbs.

Soon after the ceasefire, Jock Ferry met a local civilian who was a part-time fireman and dental technician, Mr Neville Bennett. In conversation with Jock, Neville suggested that he could provide hot baths for the men, if only he could get some form of heating oil for his domestic oil-fired central heating system. The challenge was on! We had walked past hundreds of aviation fuel drums a few days before on the outskirts of Stanley, and Jock asked Neville if this might suffice? Neville's eyes opened up, and he nodded in the affirmative, 'Yes'.

So, Jock with Neville driving the Falkland Islands short-wheel base red firefighting land-rover, set off to the fuel dump. Jock was well prepared before setting out and took with him mine-marking tape and his trusty 100m of para-cord! He ran a perimeter of mine-tape along the edge of the fuel dump, suspending some cardboard signs on announcing 'Danger – Possible Booby-traps'. He then walked up to the stash of drums, selected a couple to pull out by his para-cord. Once he was sure that they had not been booby-trapped, he rolled them towards Neville and his land-rover. Together, they lifted them onto the vehicle and set off to Neville's house. The first drum was quickly plumbed into his heating system with immediate success. Heating and hot water for the first time in weeks. The Bennett family completed their part of the deal, letting the Troop filter through their house at will, for hot drinks, and a long-welcomed bath.

The Bennett family became close friends with Jock Ferry and his wife, Sandra. So much so that when the Bennetts eventually relocated to the UK mainland, they would meet up every year. Neville died in 2021 after a long illness, and Jock was invited to play the bagpipes at his funeral, sending Neville off to the sound of 'The Crags of Tumbledown'.

The days that followed were punctuated by the arrival of more and more engineers, and the re-affiliation of 2 Troop back to our parent Squadron. For those who had been at sea since April and had landed on D-Day, there was an increasing desire to get home. News that 3 Commando Brigade were to embark on SS Canberra and

CHAPTER 14

head North without 2 Troop was hard to take. But then, a few days later, and at very short notice, we got the nod to embark on LSL Sir Geraint, which was heading for Ascension Island. With minutes to spare, the bulk of the Troop boarded, and Sir Geraint was steaming out of Port Stanley harbour.

Chapter 15

BILLY'S STORY

One member of 2 Troop had a unique experience, which deserves mention here. Steve (Billy) Morris was a 21-year-old sapper, a product of the Junior Leaders Regiment, at Old Park Barracks Dover having joined the Royal Engineers as a 16-year-old Junior Soldier in 1978. An only child, Billy was the son of a Fleet Air Arm SNCO, so his parents knew what duty and family separation was all about. Nevertheless, when the MV Norland sailed out of Portsmouth Harbour on the 26th of April 1982, they appreciated the gravity of the situation, and waved him goodbye with Union flags from the 'Sallyport', the battlements that protect the harbour entrance and have witnessed so many naval departures in years gone by. As Billy stood on the ship's port upper deck and strained to catch a glimpse of them, his Dad set off recently 'acquired' flares to mark the occasion and send him on his way.

Billy had passed the parachute training course, P Company, in September 1979. He was robust and able, a Plant Operator Mechanic by trade, and he fitted into 4 Section easily. His technical ability made him an obvious choice on the voyage South, to help operate the ship's newly fitted desalination plant, along with Sapper Grant Scott, the troop petroleum fitter.

Prior to departure, the MV Norland had undertaken an emergency major refit. Two helipads had been constructed on deck, Satnav and Satcom communications equipment had been installed and, crucially, eleven 30,000-gallon rubber water tanks had been assembled on one of the car decks to provide a desalination capability for the anticipated journey to the Falkland Islands. Operating this facility was technically demanding and time consuming. The tanks had to be balanced off to stabilise the vessel, and providing pure, clean drinking water for the 1500 people on board was technically challenging. South of Ascension Island, when the Troop cross decked onto the SS Canberra, Billy was 'volunteered' to remain on board the Norland and take over the responsibility of water supply management of the desalination plant.

From that point onwards, Billy's was to be a very different war. He had been an enthusiastic, popular and integral member of the Troop, but now he was by himself. Would he re-join the Troop? Would he be able to get ashore? What would happen to the MV Norland? All questions he asked himself. All questions with no immediate answers.

Deep in the South Atlantic, Billy now reported into the Naval Party 1850 on board the Norland. They sailed into San Carlos water on D Day, discharging 2 Para onto Red and Green beaches via Landing Ships Logistic (LSLs). He then experienced 4 very uncomfortable days in what became known as Bomb Alley, under repeated

CHAPTER 15

air raid warnings, watching bombs being dropped from Argentinian aircraft, Harriers chasing after them and Rapier missiles being launched. As one of the few on board trained to shoot, Billy was positioned high on deck with helmet on and 9mm Sub Machine Gun at the ready. One low level attack was met with Billy discharging a magazine at the approaching enemy aircraft. He knew this wasn't going to be hugely effective, but it felt good to be able to do something.

A typical 9 Squadron sapper, Billy made himself useful on board. Indeed, he became indispensable. He would be routinely called upon by the ship's first engineer to move 100 tons of water from one of the port tanks to a starboard tank or vice versa. Using a bank of pump switches and the stern loading ramp, lowered to horizontal as a kind of enormous spirit level, he would play tunes on the pillow tanks until the ship was balanced off. Once complete, he would phone the bridge, close up and seal off the loading ramp and return to his bunk. All this was done without any supervision. They just trusted him.

He was also a key member of the team when Replenishment-at-Sea (RAS) was underway. Alongside another support ship in heavy South Atlantic Sea conditions, a gun line would be fired across and then water and fuel connections made good. Billy would have to fill the pillow tanks in a particular sequence in order to ensure that the ship remained stable, opening and closing a series of valves to allow the water to flow correctly. It was intense and testing.

Returning to San Carlos Water, the Norland was alongside HMS Antelope the night it exploded and sank. The survivors boarded the Norland, and troops were dropped off ashore before the ship sailed on to South Georgia. The purpose of this voyage was to pick up members of 5 Infantry Brigade from the Queen Elizabeth the 2nd, which was thought to be too big a prize to risk in Bomb Alley. They arrived at Grytviken on the 27th of May, unloading this latest complement of re-enforcements at San Carlos 4 days later.

With the Battle of Goose Green now over, what to do with the newly captured prisoners-of-war was clearly an issue that needed to be addressed quickly. MV Norland was the obvious candidate ship to use as a prisoner-of-war vessel to get them off the Falkland Islands. A total of 1012 prisoners were embarked and secured on one of the car decks. Guarded by Royal Marines, they set sail with the prisoners-of-war thinking they were heading for England. To their surprise and delight, there destination was Uruguay. They landed at Montevideo, on the 7th of June. The Norland was met at the quayside by officials, family members and lines of buses ready to return the prisoners to Argentina. With the ship's forklift driver sick, Billy was once more utilised operating the only Eager Beaver fork-lift truck available for 9 hours solid, loading stores and victuals via the stern ramp. He had become a pivotal member of the ship's crew.

Ploughing through monumental seas, the Norland returned to San Carlos, arriving 3 days after the ceasefire,

CHAPTER 15

on the 17th of June. Collecting a further 1000 prisoners there, she sailed round to Port Stanley, picked up more POWs and left for Argentina with a complement of 2,047 Argentinians crammed on board. Landing at Puerto Madryn to a hostile reception, they disgorged the bedraggled mass of beaten soldiers onto the dock. The rear bar of the ship had been used as a medical centre for the voyage. Billy was tasked with making sure all injured soldiers were helped ashore. In one case, he had to piggy-back a young man with bad feet injuries from the ship's medical centre and down the gang plank. On the quayside, he was received by an angry crowd of families and military staff as he handed over the injured Argentinian. Not pleasant!

Billy finally returned to Port Stanley on the 23rd of June. He was desperate to be reunited with 2 Troop. He searched the town and found the guys billeted in the town's Tabernacle. With much relief, he found a space to lay down his head. Even then, his war wasn't done. He was tasked the next day with clearing mines at Stanley Airport!

I met up with Billy 37 years later and asked him about his experiences. Even after all this time, he felt raw that he had been left on board the MV Norland and that he had not been able to fight with 2 Troop in 1982. The fact that he had made a significant contribution to the conflict as an individual sapper and had conducted himself with distinction whilst on board had simply passed him by. Belonging to 2 Troop mattered much more to him.

Sapper Billy Morris, on board the MV Norland, was witness to HMS Antelope sinking in San Carlos water. Norland took on board the Antelope's surviving crew.

Armed only with a sub machine gun, Billy Morris was tasked with guard duties on MV Norland as the vessel was attacked by Argentine aircraft in San Carlos water.

Chapter 16

THE HOME FRONT

Most of 2 Troop were young single soldiers, or 'Singlies' as they were known. However, four of the Junior NCOs were married as were Sergeant Taff Sweeney and Staff Sergeant Pete Guerin. What was life like for the wives left behind in Aldershot?

Jock Ferry's wife, Sandra was perhaps typical of many wives in 9 Parachute Squadron during the summer of 1982. Sandra met Jock at the British Army Show in Aldershot in 1975. They were married three years later. By the Spring of 1982, Sandra had been an Army wife for 4 years. Their eldest boy, Gavin was born in 1982, on the 20th of January. Jock was away on exercise for 4 of the first 6 weeks of Gavin's life.

The Army community in Aldershot was close-knit. Sandra, Jock and Gavin lived on the Talavera married quarter patch, and their neighbours there included the Doyles and the Humphries. Baz and Linda Bassett also moved into Aldershot the day before the men left for Portsmouth. A small band of wives knocked on Linda's door to help her unpack her MFO boxes. All have remained friends for life. Together with Jean and Scott Wilson, they operated as one extended family. Once 2 Troop had been put on notice to deploy to the Falkland Islands,

Sandra experienced the emotional roller coaster of false starts, premature farewells, and 'on the bus, off the bus' departures. This was the experience of so many service wives that Spring. Sandra recalls that the 8th of April was her sister's 18th birthday, celebrations were to take place at her parents' house, in Leighton Buzzard. As Jock was on pre-deployment leave, this was an opportunity for them to take their new baby to meet the family.

Jock and Sandra were met on arrival by her father, somewhat stony-faced waiting at the front door. He had just been contacted by the military authorities by phone to summon Jock back to Aldershot for deployment with 2 Para. So, they abandoned the birthday celebrations, immediately turning the car round and driving back home. This proved to be one of many false starts. Amazingly, Jock had still not left Aldershot 10 days later and was able to be present at son Gavin's christening on the 18th of April. The next day, Jock packed and said goodbye (again), only to return home that evening…yet more delays!

Eventually, the Troop embarked on the MV Norland at Portsmouth the following week. The Squadron Families Officer, Captain Dick Barton, arranged for a coach for the families to journey to the port for a tearful farewell alongside the dock. Sandra has two memories of that day. Firstly, she could only see her husband, who had already embarked and was onboard the ship, from the quayside. She remembers that he shouted down to her from high up on the passenger deck, 'Treat it as an exercise. We'll be back soon!' Secondly, the Band of the Parachute Regiment was also alongside to see the battalion group off. The song

CHAPTER 16

she remembers them playing was of course 'I am sailing' by Rod Stewart, now an evocative family favourite.

The next few weeks were tense. As the Task Force sailed South, there was a growing realisation that Jock's prediction was unlikely to come true. This was to be no exercise. The sinking of the Belgrano on the 2nd of May was a turning point for many of the wives, and when HMS Sheffield was hit by an Argentinian Exocet missile two days later, it became clear that their men were likely to endure casualties. As the weeks continued, the wives developed a deep sense of camaraderie themselves. They often shared meals together, and the Squadron family lunches became important events, opportunities to share experiences, to talk and to listen and to help each other. Sandra remembers that her mother wanted her and her young son, Gavin to come and stay with them throughout the war and was most upset when she refused. The truth was that Sandra felt that Aldershot was where her friends were and where she was going to both receive and give support. It was a very exclusive club: a resilient community that looked out for everyone. Put simply, she felt that she belonged with her close-knit gang of friends in 'the Shot'.

Two events stick in Sandra's mind during those dark days. The first was immediately after hearing of 2 Para's battle at Goose Green on the 28th of May. News filtered back that this had been a tough encounter, with a number of British fatalities. For the wives in Aldershot, anticipating that 2 Para would be supported by 2 Troop, 9 Parachute Squadron, anxiety grew. They had no knowledge at this stage that the Troop had been re-assigned to under command of 3 Para.

Assembled at the Squadron Bar in Montgomery lines, they waited for Squadron Rear Party and Families Officer, Captain Dick Barton to return to the meal, after being notified that there was a signal in the Squadron offices with news of the engagement. This was Dick's first tour with the Squadron, so when he learnt that the only sapper fatality at Goose Green was Corporal Mick Melia, from 59 Independent Commando Squadron, he thought this news would be greeted with relief by the assembled wives. He was not to know that Mick Melia had recently been posted from 9 Parachute Squadron in Aldershot to Plymouth to join the sister Squadron. Mick and his wife, Gill, were hugely popular members of the 2 Troop community during their time in Aldershot. Poor Dick Barton was devasted when he learnt of Mick Melia's close association with 9 Squadron.

The second event that sticks in Sandra's mind was, of course, the Battle for Mount Longdon. At the time, Sandra and the other wives were still unaware of where the Troop was and which battalion they were operating with. Whilst Longdon was a baptism of fire for 2 Troop, it was in many ways just as hard for the wives back in Aldershot. With little information available apart from the monotone voice of Ian McDonald, Ministry of Defence spokesman on the BBC News each evening, all they could do was wait and try and keep busy. On the night of the 13th of June, Sandra was contacted by Dick Barton. He had bad news to give to Jean Wilson, and he needed to make sure that Jean had friends at hand to support her. Sandra duly assembled outside Jean's house with close friends Leslie Doyle and Chris Humphries. Dick sat with Jean by herself in the

CHAPTER 16

lounge and informed her that Scott had been killed. Her friends waited in the hallway until the awful message had been delivered. According to Sandra, Jean immediately phoned Gill Melia in Plymouth to let her know that she wasn't on her own in her bereavement. Jean's sister, Linda came round and asked the girls to stay with Jean until she could pack her overnight bag and return. Tragically, little did Linda know then that her own husband, Corporal Ginge McCarthy, from Support Company, 3 Para, had also been killed a few minutes earlier on the same mountain during the same battle.

Jean and Scott Wilson were married in 1980. They had met in the Royal Exchange pub in Aldershot two years previously and had endured four months separation soon after their marriage, when 9 Squadron were sent on a tour of duty in Northern Ireland in 2000/01. Jean's sister, Linda married Corporal Keith McCarthy a few weeks before the Falklands campaign. Keith was known as Ginge to his friends and colleagues, and was a key member of the Milan Platoon, 3rd Battalion, The Parachute Regiment (3 Para). As Ginge deployed to the Falklands with 3 Para and Scott's Troop was supporting 2 Para, Jean made the reasonable assumption that they would not be serving together during the conflict. But once 2 Troop had been re-assigned to support 3 Para, this proved to be a devastatingly inaccurate assumption to make.

Jean recalls that, once the menfolk had left Aldershot, the wives stuck very close together. Jean remembers helping her sister redecorate her new married quarter, partly to keep busy and keep minds occupied.

Etched forever in Jean's mind is the memory of Families Officer, Dick Barton's visit on the 13th of June and her realisation that Scott had been killed. Understandably, she describes the events immediately afterwards as just 'a blur'. She remembers Dick's kindness, compassion, sensitivity and dignity, and her fellow wives supporting her as she came to terms with the news of Scott's death. Breaking the news to family in Scotland and Kuwait was harrowing for her. And then came the news of her brother-in-law, Ginge McCarthy's death which Jean's sister received two days later. The sisters had lost both their husbands on the same battlefield within minutes of each other.

For Squadron Rear Party and Families Officer Dick Barton, the summer of 1982 proved to be highly challenging. Dick was a hugely likeable and bubbly character who had completed the parachute training course somewhat late in his career. Underneath his fit, tough exterior lay a gentle, caring and compassionate disposition. He was posted to 9 Parachute Squadron for the first time as the Admin Officer. This appointment brought with it the additional roles as Rear Party and Families Officer when the Squadron went to war. Like most unit Families Officers, Dick had no previous experience of dealing with families whose loved ones were in a conflict zone. On commissioning two years previously, he received a limited amount of training on the subject but for the most part, he had to use his wits and his twenty-five years of military experience to see him through.

Without any guidance from more senior officers, Dick threw himself into the task of looking after the wives in the best way he could. Typically, on Airborne

CHAPTER 16

Forces Day, he organised a wives sponsored parachute jump, co-opting Captain Micky Mann and the Red Devils Parachute Display Team to help. Several wives including Sandra Ferry and Chris Humphries took part, plus Dick himself and Dick's daughter, Tina. Amusingly, one of the wives managed to complete a parachute jump before her husband, who had left for the Falklands before he could complete his parachute training.

Dick, ably supported by the Squadron Rear Party, organised weekly lunches and other events to keep the wives both busy and informed. Dick was sensitive that bad news from the South Atlantic looked increasingly likely, so he made an unwritten agreement with them. The deal was that he would never go onto the married quarters patch unless he was bringing bad news. The point was that he didn't want them unnecessarily anxious or upset every time they saw him visiting the married quarters. Forty years on, what is clear is that the wives really appreciated Dick's efforts. Jean Wilson and Sandra Ferry have nothing but praise for the way he conducted himself during those enormously difficult months.

2 Troop was honoured when Jean Wilson agreed to attend their Falklands Dinner on their return to Aldershot, in August 1982. On reflection, it must have been immensely difficult for her to see the entire Troop gathered with wives and girlfriends. Whilst all were sensitive to the situation, there were expressions of relief, joy and pride that night about what the Troop had achieved. Looking back, we were not as sensitive to Jean's sad situation as we should have been. So, when we met

up via a Teams call last year, I asked her how she felt about that evening. Jean said that she found it cathartic to be with Scott's friends and colleagues. Her words were 'It made me feel that I belonged to 2 Troop. I wanted to be treated as part of the family.'

Forty years on, it's hard to fully understand the enormity of the grief that fell upon the married quarters in Aldershot that June. There is no doubt that for Jean Wilson, these were defining moments in her life. Like all the Squadron wives, she remains intensely proud of her husband and what he achieved – Sandra Ferry remains equally proud of her band of wives who stuck together, held each other in mourning their dead, and supported each other as they awaited news. Sandra recounts that the Talavera married quarters developed a code of conduct around not knocking on each other's doors that summer. For a knock at the front door, often meant bad news. So, they agreed to knock on the window instead. Even the postman was trained accordingly!

In the weeks after the Battle for Mount Longdon, the focus turned to whether Scott Wilson's body would be repatriated or not. It had long been a tradition in the British Army that the dead were buried in the theatre of operations where they fell, but pressure mounted immediately after the Falklands conflict for close family to be given a choice. Bodies would be repatriated if requested by Next-Of-Kin. For Jean, there was a real desire to have her husband brought home. And so it came to pass that Scott was buried with full military honours in Edinburgh that December. His coffin was towed on a gun carriage

CHAPTER 16

by airborne Land Rover along Princess Street, escorted by his best friend, Jock Ferry, who gave the Eulogy that day. Scott was buried and still lies in Easter Road Cemetery.

Captain Dick Barton, Admin Officer and Families Officer 9 Parachute Squadron, and his dog, Louey – 1982.

9 Parachute Squadron wives prepare for their charity parachute jump with the Red Devils. May 1982.

CHAPTER 16

Jock, Sandra and Gavin Ferry on the bus home to Aldershot from RAF Brize Norton.

Chapter 17

THE RETURN HOME

Landing Ships Logistic, or LSL's, are flat bottomed vessels designed to be able to undertake beach landings if necessary. They don't perform well in rough weather. As we were to discover, they don't perform well at all in Force 11 gales in the South Atlantic. Boarding the LSL Sir Geraint[1] at Port Stanley was a huge relief for the whole Troop. For three days, the wind kept blowing and the ship kept shuddering as wave after wave hit it. Everyone was bedded down. No food was eaten. But we didn't care. We had survived and we were on our way home.

After 2 years with 2 Troop, I had learnt that their irrepressible spirit was matched with an insatiable appetite to be either creative or mischievous, or sometimes both. After 3 days at sea in the South Atlantic, the weather began to improve. Sea sickness abated. The guys decided that their 'cruise ship' needed a swimming pool. So they built one using old pallets, and tifor jacks. They strapped the pallets to the ship's deck using the tirfor jacks and wire hawser, and then lined the luxury swimming pool with the plastic membrane.

---

1 I think it was the Sir Geraint, but 40 years on, I cannot be sure!

BELONGING TO 2 TROOP

Although it didn't survive the initial lumpy sea conditions and had to be rebuilt twice, it proved a constant source of entertainment in the last few days on board.

At Ascension, we disembarked and became hostage to the Royal Corps of Transport's Movement organisation, awaiting an RAF VC 10 to fly us into RAF Brize Norton. It was whilst waiting that we were encouraged by the Movement Staff to hand over any contraband we had acquired. Substantial quantities of Argentinian weapons, night sights and personal equipment were stacked up, enough to equip a small army.

Not many of the Troop had ever seen the Royal Engineers Corps Band before. None had ever experienced it playing for us. But there it was on the tarmac at RAF Brize Norton, together with the Deputy Engineer-in-Chief, to welcome us home. Perhaps it was only then, or shortly afterwards, when we were released from customs to meet family and friends, that the enormity of what we had achieved was brought home to us.

One member of the Troop had no-one to welcome him at RAF Brize Norton. Lance Corporal Derek Broadbent said goodbye to his comrades, walked through the arrivals lounge and out of the main gate. He then thumbed a lift to Plymouth, dressed in his combat uniform and with his Bergan strapped to his back. It was late evening on the 11th of July 1982. He was dropped off, made his way to his parent's house and knocked on the door. His war had ended. He was home.

That afternoon, having returned to their families, some in the Troop may have sneaked a view on television of the tick-a-tape welcome in Southampton water, as SS Canberra returned home, victorious. The whole of 3

CHAPTER 17

Commando Brigade was on board. It was a spectacular scene as Canberra was escorted by an armada of small ships. The quayside was bursting with families and well-wishers. The emotional homecoming was transmitted live to a huge national television audience. One or two in the Troop might have been a little envious. But then again, the ship was full of marines. 2 Troop didn't belong there!

For me personally, the wedding that was postponed in May finally took place on the 7th of August that year in Great Coxwell, Oxfordshire. Mandy and I still live in the village, next to the church where we were married.

Mandy and I finally got hitched on the 7th of August 1982. The guard of honour included Freddie Kemp, 2IC 9 Parachute Squadron, Dick Barton, the Squadron's Families Officer, and Richard Willett, 1 Troop Commander in the Falklands.

BELONGING TO 2 TROOP

From: Major R Macdonald RE
                                        59 Independent Commando Squadron RE
                                        Operation Corporate
                                        British Forces Post Office 666

Lieutenant Colonel G W Field MBE RE
Commander Royal Engineers
Falkland Islands   25 June 1982

Dear Robbie — for your personal info only.

2 Troop 9 Parachute Squadron have been directly under my command since 7 May 1982, through a campaign that has been a test of everything that makes up a soldier and a unit.

Their performance as a troop has in every respect been quite outstanding. On 21 May they went ashore in Port San Carlos in support of 3 PARA. They patrolled intensively, constructed a water point, busied themselves improving tracks and defensive positions and started construction of the Harrier Pad. During this period LCpl Hare was wounded, on patrol.

On 27 May they marched, carrying their kit, with 3 PARA to Teal Inlet. From Teal they again marched to Mount Challenger where they established a water point and took part in some particularly hard patrolling in the Mount Longdon area establishing safe routes for the assault on Mount Longdon. The conditions on Mount Challenger were wet, windswept and very cold, at all times they remained cheerful and resiliant.

On 12 June they assaulted Mount Longdon in support of 3 PARA. This proved to be a most difficult and tough battle, probably the hardest of that night. They were under continual shell, mortar and direct fire. It was at this time Cpl Wilson was killed by shell fire. The troop was employed clearing enemy positions and some mines. For over 24 hours they were continually shelled and mortared.

On 14 June they supported 3 PARA again in their assault on Stanley as back up for 2 PARA. On arrival in Stanley they assumed responsibility for clearing the main town, a task which they tackled with relish, quickly establishing a good relationship with the local people.

2 Troop 9 Parachute Squadron have been an exemplary standard bearer for their most famous squadron. I have been proud to command them during this operation, they have given their all and as a result are greatly respected by all ranks within my squadron. They have done a great deal to establish even closer ties between our two specialist squadrons.

I thank you for loaning them to me during this most astonishing operation. They return to you with honour.
I enclose an insert slip for Captain Burn's confidential report signed by the Commander 3 Commando Brigade.

Yours aye,

Roderick

Letter written by Major Roddy Macdonald to Lieutenant Colonel Geoff Field, CO 36 Engineer Regiment at the end of hostilities, in June 1982. Although in 1982 this copy was intended for the author's personal information only, Roddy Macdonald has agreed that it can be included in this account of 2 Troop's story.

CHAPTER 17

Majors Roddy Macdonald, OC 59 Independent Commando Squadron and Chris Davies, OC 9 Parachute Squadron, Royal Engineers.

Photo taken on Stanley airfield after the surrender.

Chapter 18

REFLECTIONS

The Troop returned to Barracks in July 1982, took some leave and for many, life resumed as normal. I was immediately posted to Germany as Second-in-Command 10 Field Squadron, Royal Engineers in Gutersloh. I didn't see any of the Troop for several years. Some might say that, for whatever reason, we never really received the recognition we deserved for our part in the Falklands campaign. In truth, our remarkable story was understood and fully recognised by Major Roddy Macdonald, our Officer Commanding during the campaign. I include in this memoir a copy of his letter to Lieutenant Colonel Geoff Field, written on the 25th of June 1982, as the Troop was returned to the command of 9 Parachute Squadron. I include it as Troop members will not have seen it before and may not have appreciated how we were regarded by our Officer Commanding during the Falklands campaign.

Monday the 5th of November 2007 was an icy cold day. Twenty-five years had passed since the Falklands War. I was now a civilian, having resigned from the British Army as Brigadier, and had forged a new career in the rail industry. I was heading to Grantham in Lincolnshire that day for a funeral. Staff Sergeant Pete Guerin had died, taken too early at the age of 63. As I approached the church, I wondered if any of the guys from 2 Troop might also make the journey. After all, I thought, it's a miserable day and Lincolnshire isn't the most accessible place to get to. It would be the start of a busy working week for many.

I need not have worried. As I parked up, there, outside the church was the whole Troop, resplendent in their red berets and sporting their campaign medals.

What was clear that day was that rank or status didn't matter anymore. Nor was there any competitiveness about how well each of us had or had not done in the intervening years. What mattered was that we were together again to honour Pete and to support his family. But beyond that, there was a sense of belonging too. Belonging to that other family that was 2 Troop.

REFERENCES

1. Friendly fire in the Falklands – Dr AD Chissel.
2. Three Days in June – James O'Connell.
3. 3 Commando Brigade in the Falklands – No Picnic – Julian Thompson.
4. Men of the Red Beret – Max Arthur.
5. Ready for Anything – Julian Thompson.
6. The Falklands War – The Sunday Times.
7. A memoir of 9 Parachute Squadron Royal Engineers in the Falklands Campaign 1982 – CM Davies MBE.
8. Logistics in the Falklands War. A case study in expeditionary warfare. Kenneth L Privratsky.
9. Battle for the Falklands. Max Hastings.
10. A Falklands Family at War. Neville and Valerie Bennett.
11. MV Norland. Secret Weapon of the Falklands War. Reg Kemp and Michael Wood.
12. With 3 Para to the Falklands. Graham Colbeck.
13. Falklands War Operational Manual. Haynes.

2 Troop, 9 Parachute Squadron, Royal Engineers.

APRIL – JULY 1982

TROOP HEADQUARTERS

Capt Robbie Burns, SSgt Pete Guerin, Sgt Taff Sweeney, L/Cpl Derek Broadbent, Sprs Mick Beeby and Kev Lillicrap.

A SECTION

Cpl John Ferry, L/Cpl John Hare, Sprs Bob Chatterton, John Chetwynd, Tony Craven, Martin (Spike) Glover, Steve (Billy) Morris, Scouse Murray, Pete Polson, Dave Raes, Scouse Smith and John Stubbs.

B SECTION

Cpl Scott Wilson, L/Cpls Paul (Ginge) Moore, Jonah Jones, Steve Wildman, Sprs Semi Lobban, Spud Murphy, Gillie Poulter, Taff Preston, Sam Robson, Scottie Scott and Mark Thistlewhite.

C SECTION

Cpl Kev Cowling, L/Cpls Mick Humphries, Steve Gabbitas, Taff Smith, Sprs Gary (Titch) Fortuin, Percy Purcell, Dillwyn Rogers, Smythe Taylor, Steve Tickle and Tommy Trindall.

SUPPORT SECTION

Cpl Bob Wilson, Cpl Brummie Lynock, L/Cpls Ginge Hall, Mick Leather, Ginge Lincoln, Sprs Clark, Thomas, John Hart, Willy McDonald, Jack Meldrum and Paddy Naylor.

My thanks to some old soldiers and their wives for helping me write this memoir.

Taff Sweeny

Jock Ferry

Mick Humphries

Steve (Billy) Morris and Mick Leather

Sandra Ferry and Chris Humphries

Derek Broadbent

Ginge Moore